THE PHILOSOPHY OF LEIBNIZ

NICHOLAS RESCHER

Professor of Philosophy
University of Pittsburgh

PRENTICE-HALL, INC., *Englewood Cliffs, New Jersey*

*Its author dedicates the book to his colleague,
friend, and helpful critic*

NUEL D. BELNAP, JR.

Current printing (last digit):
10 9 8 7 6 5 4 3 2 1

Library of Congress Catalog Card No.: 66-29698
Printed in the United States of America (66386-C)

PRENTICE-HALL INTERNATIONAL, INC., *London*
PRENTICE-HALL OF AUSTRALIA, PTY. LTD., *Sydney*
PRENTICE-HALL OF CANADA, LTD., *Toronto*
PRENTICE-HALL OF INDIA (PRIVATE) LTD., *New Delhi*
PRENTICE-HALL OF JAPAN, INC., *Tokyo*

PREFACE

The aim of this book is to give a systematic introduction to the philosophy of Leibniz—a synoptic picture that is historically faithful and substantively coherent and cogent. In providing this account, we seek to navigate in the narrow channel between the Scylla of uncritical exposition and the Charybdis of loose interpretation and hasty critique.

Leibniz' philosophy not only can, but must be viewed *as a system,* an intricate, unified structure which, like the rococo decorations of his time, he worked out with almost endless attention to detail. It is this writer's considered opinion that Leibniz' prodigious intellectual labors and the quality of his philosophical workmanship polished his system into an unusually diversified yet coherent whole. The surface inconsistencies which later critics have reproved with such facility are generally found, on closer inspection, not to be there at all. An *internal* critique of Leibniz' philosophy on grounds of intrinsic incongruities and inconsistencies must, I believe, be a relatively unrewarding venture. Insofar as Leibniz' philosophy is unacceptable—and this is something which cannot at this time be doubted—it is because of the unacceptability of its premises, not because of inconsistencies in the way in which the system is worked out from its basic commitments.

No compact presentation of Leibniz can convey an adequate idea of the enormous diversity and richness of his philosophical writings. He never actually wrote one systematic treatise presenting his "system," but revealed it piece by piece in the course of innumerable articles, letters, and papers. This endows his philosophical exposition with a uniquely prismatic character, each of the major ideas being a *leitmotiv* that repeatedly comes to the fore from a great variety of perspectives.

It is necessary to say a brief word of the indebtedness of the present book to some of my earlier publications. Leibniz is one of my philosophical heroes, and I have long been intrigued by the logico-mathematical rigor of his philosophizing. My Princeton doctoral dissertation on "Leibniz' Cosmology," written just 15 years ago, provides much of the material for Chapters Seven and Eight of this book. An article, which was worked out as a followup to this dissertation, on "Contingence in the Philosophy of Leibniz" [*The Philosophical Review*, Vol. 6 (1952), 26-39], furnished material for Chapter Four.

I am indebted to the students in a Leibniz seminar given at the University of Pittsburgh during the Fall trimester of 1965 for their comments on a draft version of this book. Professor Leroy E. Loemker of Emory University has read the material in preliminary form and enabled me to profit by his comments and criticisms. I also wish to thank Miss Dorothy Henle and Betty (Mrs. Arthur) Laubach for producing, through several versions, a typescript of the material suitable for the printer's use. I am grateful to Miss Henle and to Anne (Mrs. Michael) Pelon for helping to see the book through the press.

N. R.

Pittsburgh
December, 1965

CONTENTS

introduction

LEIBNIZ' LIFE AND WORKS

This introductory discussion will be divided into two separate parts. The first attempts to give a general picture of Leibniz' life and writings, the second presents a summary overview of the Leibniz literature.

Leibniz' Life and Writings

Gottfried Wilhelm von Leibniz was born on July 1, 1646, at Leipzig, where his father was professor of moral philosophy at the university. He attended school for a time, but after his father's death in 1652 studied at home, and was largely self-taught from the German and Latin books of his father's library, in addition to teaching himself to read Greek. Early in his teens he began an intensive study of logic, scholastic philosophy, and Protestant theology. At 15 he entered the University of Leipzig as a law student. During the first preparatory years, one semester of which he spent at Jena, he studied principally philosophy, natural philosophy, and mathematics. His baccalaureate dissertation of 1663 (*De principio individui*) was devoted to a subject—the principle of individuation—to which he was to give lifelong attention. The next three years were devoted to legal studies, and in 1666 Leibniz applied for the degree of doctor of law. As he was but 20 years of age, his application was rejected on the grounds of youth by the university of his native city, but was immediately granted at the University of Altdorf (near Nuremberg), where his highly original dissertation "On Difficult Problems in the Law" (*De casibus perplexis in jure*) secured him the offer of a university position. This he declined, his goal being to enter public rather than academic life.

Before reaching 21, Leibniz had not only earned his doctorate in law, but had published several original studies in logic and legal theory. The presence of such a prodigy in Nuremberg was brought to the attention of Baron Johann Christian von Boineburg (1622–1672), former Prime Minister to the elector of Mainz, and one of the most prominent political figures in Germany. Through his aid, Leibniz entered the service of the elector of Mainz. Apart from official missions, all the rest of his life was spent in residence at various courts.

At Mainz he was set to work on writings of a political nature. The most important was a memorandum for Louis XIV suggesting that Holland, as a merchant power with extensive trade in the East, might be seriously injured through the conquest of Egypt (a scheme which would incidentally serve Germany's interests by diverting French expansionism from Europe). Nothing came of the project at the time, but the idea seems to have stayed alive in French official circles until it came to fruition in the time of Napoleon. In 1672, Leibniz was sent to Paris in the elector's service to promote the Egyptian scheme. Although the mission failed to realize its objective, it, and a trip Leibniz made to London in conjunction with it, proved crucially important for Leibniz' intellectual development, for he now came into direct contact with the wider world of European learning.

In 1672, when Leibniz was 26, Descartes' followers and disciples were in possession of the philosophical arena, and some who had personally known and corresponded with him were still active [e.g., Thomas Hobbes (1588–1679)]. Leibniz was able to establish personal contact with such important Cartesian followers as Antoine Arnauld (1612–1694), Nicholas Melebranche (1636–1715), and

Spinoza (1632–1677), whom Leibniz visited in the Netherlands in 1675. Spinoza and John Locke (1632–1704) were still young. Modern physical science was in its lusty infancy. Robert Boyle (1627–1691) still had many years before him. Isaac Newton (1642–1727), with whom Leibniz was to enter into a fateful correspondence, was only at the beginning of his career. The mathematician-physicist Huygens (1629–1695) became Leibniz' mentor and friend in the course of the Paris visit. The scientific firmament was replete with such luminaries as von Guerike, Mariotte, Papin, and Perrault in physics, van Leeuwenhoek in biology, and the Bernouillis, Sturm, Wallis, and Varignon in mathematics; and Leibniz entered into contact and correspondence with virtually all of them. (He came to collect correspondents on scientific topics as another man might collect rare books.) The doors to this far-flung realm of European learning were first opened to Leibniz in the course of his Parisian mission.

In January, 1673, Leibniz traveled to London as attaché on a political mission for the elector of Mainz. There he became acquainted with H. Oldenburg, Secretary of the Royal Society, and others of its members. He exhibited to the Royal Society a calculating machine of his own devising, more versatile than the earlier machine of Pascal. In April, 1673, shortly after returning to Paris, Leibniz was elected a fellow of the Royal Society. In Paris he devoted himself intensively to higher mathematics, especially geometry, largely under the tutelage of Huygens, and at this point began a series of original studies that culminated in his invention of the differential and integral calculus.

While in Paris, Leibniz transferred from the service of the elector of Mainz to that of Duke John Frederick of Brunswick-Lüneburg. In 1675 he settled in Hanover at the Duke's request, traveling there via London and Amsterdam, where he held conversations with Spinoza, of whose (then unpublished) *Ethics* he was able to make notes.

For the 40 remaining years of his active life Leibniz continued—under three successive princes—in the service of the Brunswick family. He was, as it were, a minister-without-portfolio in charge of historico-political, cultural, and scientific affairs. He wrote tracts to justify various rights and claims of the dukes of Hanover, and he superintended the mint and reorganized the mines. Though he lived in the atmosphere of petty politics in a small German principality, his interests and outlook were always wide-ranging and international. From 1687 to 1690 he traveled extensively through Germany and Italy, searching public records and archives to gather material for an official history of the house of Brunswick. After returning from Italy in 1690, Leibniz was made librarian of the ducal library at Wolfenbüttel by Duke Anton of Brunswick-Wolfenbüttel.

In the next years Leibniz concentrated his official efforts on his history of the house of Brunswick (which at his death had gone no further than the period 768–1005) and organized material collected in his travels for a code of international law into two books. He established connections at the court of Berlin, and used his influence to promote the establishment there in 1700 of the royal academy (*Akademie der Wissenschaften*), of which he was elected president for life. Founding academies modeled on those of Paris and London was a favorite project with Leibniz. He urged upon Peter the Great the plan for an academy at St. Petersburg which was not carried out until after the czar's death. In the course of an official visit to Vienna from 1712–1714 he promoted (unsuccessfully) a plan for establishing an academy there. This Viennese visit did give Leibniz great satisfaction, however, for he received the honor of an imperial Privy Councillorship and a Barony of the Empire.

Upon the death of Queen Anne in August, 1714, Leibniz' master, the elector George Louis of Hanover, succeeded to the throne of England as King George I. Leibniz returned to Hanover by September, but George had already departed for England. Leibniz was eager to follow him to London and play a greater role on a larger stage, but the feeling against him in England ran high in the wake of the priority dispute over the calculus between his adherents and Newton's. Leibniz was ordered to remain at Hanover and finish his history of the house of Brunswick, working in the vacuum left by the general exodus of important courtiers. He died on November 14, 1716, his last years made difficult by neglect, illness, and the distrust of the local public. (The Hanover clergy called him *"Lövenix"*—believer in nothing—and his reputation as an unbeliever made him locally unpopular.) Despite this, he retained to the end his capacity for hard work in pursuit of active researches in many fields of learning.

Leibniz possessed an astounding range of interests and capacities. Mathematics, physics, geology, philosophy, logic, philology, theology, history, jurisprudence, politics, and economics are all subjects to which he made original contributions of the first rank. The universality of the range of his abilities and achievements is without rival in modern time.

By prodigious energy, ability, and effort, Leibniz managed to be three persons in one—a scholar, a public servant and man of affairs, and a courtier—without letting any one suffer at the expense of the others. He possessed amazing powers for swift and sustained work, sometimes taking meals at his desk and spending days on end there, except for a few occasional hours of sleep. Even while traveling in the rough conveyances of the day he worked at mathematical problems.

In contemporary accounts Leibniz is described as a man of moderate habits, quick in temper but easily appeased, very self-assured, and impatient of contradiction, his irascibility no doubt the result of chronic overwork. By all evidence he was a man of wise understanding in human affairs, wide-ranging in interests, charitable in judgment of others, and tolerant of differences in customs and opinions. Leibniz' interests imbued him with a thoroughly cosmopolitan point of view. In discussing resumption of the work of the French Academy after the Peace of Ryswick (1697) he wrote:

> Provided that something of consequence is achieved, I am indifferent whether this is done in Germany or in France, for I seek the good of mankind. I am neither a *phil-Hellene* nor a *philo-Roman,* but a *phil-anthropos.*[1]

Leibniz loved to mingle with people in society and hoped to learn something from everyone. His secretary said that he spoke well of everybody and made the best of everything. He is said to have been money conscious and tightfisted. He was perhaps overanxious to secure the recognition and honor he believed due him for his work and services. In learned controversy in correspondence he was incredibly patient and good tempered.

A word must be said about Leibniz' philosophical development. Until he was 15 or 16, he was under the influence of the scholastics whose works he read in his father's library. In the course of his studies of the sciences at the University he inclined to a materialistic atomism (of the sort to be found in Gassendi and Bacon), a posi-

---

[1] *Phil.,* VII, p. 456.

tion from which he was moved in the early 1670's by a complicated complex of anti-materialist influences. (Leibniz' thought was molded by a diversified multitude of thinkers whose influence will perhaps never be unraveled; among the ancients are the Platonic tradition and Plato himself; among the medievals, the scholastics as well as the "new" Aristotle; in the Renaissance, Nicholas of Cusa and the entire Platonic movement of the late Renaissance; among the moderns, the Atomists, Bacon, and Hobbes.) The rudiments of his monadism were conceived by 1675, but for the long interval 1675–1685 Leibniz devoted himself mainly to his official duties and to mathematics, logic, and physics. His ideas in metaphysics lay fallow, apart from his continued intensive assimilation of ideas—the influence on Leibniz of Hobbes and Descartes was now prominent, albeit largely by way of negation. However, it was as much the effect of his devotion to mathematics and physics as of any purely philosophical influences that turned him away from his early atomistic leanings. During the winter of 1685–1686 he returned to philosophy and, in a concentrated period of thought, worked out the details of his philosophical system and wrote several superficial sketches of it (primarily the *Discourse on Metaphysics*). I think it fair to say that as of 1686 Leibniz' philosophy had reached its mature completion, and all of his subsequent writing on the subject can be looked upon as exposing to public view further parts of an existing structure to which little or no substantial additions, in more than expository and ornamental detail, are being made.

The story of Leibniz' philosophical writings is complex. He published only one philosophical book, the *Essais de Théodicée* (1710), although he wrote a second, the *Nouveaux Essais sur l'Entendement Humain,* a critique of John Locke's *An Essay Concerning Human Understanding,* which he left unpublished upon Locke's death in 1704. The essence of Leibniz' mature philosophy was contained in a series of occasional articles he published between 1686 and 1716 in such journals as the *Acta Eruditorum* of Leipzig and the *Journal des Savants* of Paris. But behind these generally sketchy articles lay a vast series of essays and memoranda prepared for personal use and never put into form for publication. The format Leibniz selected for propagation of his ideas was letters to select correspondents. (It would seem he was less concerned about publishing his system for the world than securing the adhesion, or at any rate understanding, of a score or two of leading intellects.) It is from the personal memoranda and his vast correspondence that one is able to obtain a firm and balanced grasp upon his philosophical system: the published works are but a window through which one can glance into the various parts of a larger structure. *Qui me non nisi editis novit, non novit,*[2] Leibniz very properly wrote on one occasion.

The Leibniz Literature

As indicated by the preceding discussion, Leibniz was a compulsive writer. Letters, memoranda, drafts, and essays flowed from his pen in an endless stream, and only a small fraction of this mass of material was put into print during his lifetime. He could not bring himself to throw written material away, and after his death his papers were collected in packing crates in the Royal Library of Hanover. This material is described in detail in

Edward Bodemann, *Die Leibniz—Handschriften der königlichen öffentlichen Bibliothek zu Hanover.* Hanover: Hahn, 1895.

Gradually, as generations of Leibniz scholars edited and published material, a more solid and rounded appreciation of the range and depth of his work became possible.

A complete bibliography of all of Leibniz' writings that had found their way into print until 1935 is

Emile Ravier, *Bibliographie des Oeuvres de Leibniz.* Paris: Felix Alcan, 1937.

In 1900 an agreement was reached between the Prussian and French academies that a complete edition of Leibniz' writings should be undertaken. Four German and four French scholars were entrusted with the preliminary task of surveying the manuscripts in the royal library at Hanover. The joint project aborted during World War I, but after the war the Prussian Academy decided to proceed with a complete Leibniz edition (*Sämtliche Schriften und Briefe*) in six series: I. Historical and Political Correspondence, II. Philosophical Correspondence, III. Scientific Correspondence, IV. Historical and Political Writings, V. Scientific Writings, and VI. Philosophical Writings. A few volumes in several of these series

---

2 "One who knows me only by the published works, does not know me at all."

LEIBNIZ' LIFE AND WORKS / 8

appeared in the interwar period, but the project ground to a halt in Nazi times. (A few volumes prepared before the war were issued afterwards.) In the course of World War II the manuscript materials became scattered; most material that had been in Berlin for the Academy edition came into the possession of East Germany, and some of the Hanover material went to other libraries for safekeeping. Arrangements are currently underway among scholarly institutions in East and West Germany for continuation of the Academy edition, and one further volume of Series VI has been prepared for publication in the Leibniz Forschungsstelle in Münster with the collaboration of André Robinet of France.

Until this elaborate project is advanced, the principal instrument with which the student of Leibniz' philosophy will have to work is

C. I. Gerhardt, *Die philosophischen Schriften von G. W. Leibniz,* 7 vols. Berlin: Weidmann, 1875-1890.

Other editions especially useful for particular subject-matter regions follow.

Leibniz' work in mathematics and physics:

C. I. Gerhardt, *Leibnizens mathematische Schriften,* 7 vols. Berlin and Halle: Weidmann, 1850–1863.

Leibniz' historical and political writings:

Onno Klopp, *Die Werke von Leibniz . . . Erste Reihe: Historisch-politische und staatswissenschaftliche Schriften,* 11 vols. Hanover: Klindworth, 1864–1884.

Leibniz' logic:

Louis Couturat, *Opuscules et fragments inédits de Leibniz.* Paris: Felix Alcan, 1903.

Leibniz' physical and technological writings:

Ernst Gerland, *Leibnizens nachgelassene Schriften physikalischen, mechanischen und technischen Inhalts.* Leipzig: B. G. Teubner, 1906.

Leibniz' ethics and theology:

Gaston Grua, *G. W. Leibniz: Textes inédits,* 2 vols. Paris: Presses Universitaires de France, 1948.
————, *Jurisprudence universelle et théodicée selon Leibniz.* Paris: Presses Universitaires de France, 1953.
————, *La justice human selon Leibniz.* Paris: Presses Universitaires de France, 1956.

The principal English translation of Leibniz' philosophical works is

L. E. Loemker, *Leibniz: Philosophical Papers and Letters*, 2 vols. Chicago: University of Chicago Press, 1956. The Introduction of this work contains a useful bibliography of the Leibniz literature, more complete than the compact overview given here.

Other English versions, some of which have special points of merit, are:

H. G. Alexander, *The Leibniz-Clarke Correspondence*. Manchester: Manchester University Press, 1956.
J. M. Child, *The Early Mathematical Manuscripts of Leibniz*. La Salle, Ill.: Open Court Publishing Co., 1920.
G. M. Duncan, *G. W. Leibniz: Works*, 2d ed. New Haven: Tuttle, Morehouse & Taylor Co., 1908.
E. M. Huggard, *G. W. Leibniz: Theodicy*. London: Routledge & Kegan Paul, 1952.
A. G. Langley, *New Essays Concerning Human Understanding by G. W. Leibniz*, 2d ed. La Salle, Ill.: Open Court Publishing Co., 1916. Has numerous notes and an excellent index. The appendices contain some of Leibniz' physical writings.
R. Latta, *Leibniz: The Monadology and Other Philosophical Writings*. London: Oxford University Press, 1898.
P. Lucas and L. Grint, *G. W. Leibniz: Discourse on Metaphysics*. Manchester: Manchester University Press, 1952.
G. R. Montgomery, *Leibniz: Discourse on Metaphysics and Correspondence with Arnauld*. La Salle, Ill.: Open Court Publishing Co., 1902. Revised by A. R. Chandler in 1924.
M. Morris, *The Philosophical Writings of G. W. Leibniz*. London: J. M. Dent & Sons, Ltd., 1934.
C. W. Russell, *G. W. Leibniz: A System of Theology*. London: James Burns, 1850.
P. P. Wiener, *Leibniz: Selections*. New York: Charles Scribner's Sons, 1951.

The most important secondary works on Leibniz' philosophy are:

Ernest Cassirer, *Leibniz' System*. Marburg an der Lahn: N. G. Elwert, 1902; photoreprinted, Hildesheim, 1962.
Louis Couturat, *La logique de Leibniz*. Paris: Felix Alcan, 1901.
Bertrand Russell, *A Critical Exposition of the Philosophy of Leibniz*. Cambridge: University of Cambridge Press, 1900. Second edition, London: George Allen & Unwin, Ltd., 1937.

Some other works available in English warrant listing:

H. W. Carr, *Leibniz*. London: Ernest Benn, Ltd., 1929; reprinted, New York: Dover Publications, 1960.

H. W. B. Joseph, *Lectures on the Philosophy of Leibniz.* Oxford: Clarendon Press, 1949.

Gottfried Martin, *Leibniz: Logic and Metaphysics,* Tr. K. J. Northcott and P. G. Lucas. Manchester: Manchester University Press, 1963.

G. H. R. Parkinson, *Logic and Reality in Leibniz' Metaphysics.* Oxford: Clarendon Press, 1965.

R. L. Saw, *Leibniz.* London: Penguin Books, 1954.

A. T. Tymieniecka, *Leibniz' Cosmological Synthesis.* Assen: Van Gorcum, 1964.

R. M. Yost, Jr., *Leibniz and Philosophical Analysis.* Berkeley and Los Angeles: University of California Press, 1954.

A work not specifically devoted to Leibniz, but nevertheless providing very useful background for the student of his philosophy, is

A. O. Lovejoy, *The Great Chain of Being.* Cambridge, Mass.: Harvard University Press, 1936.

The classic and most authoritative biography of Leibniz is

G. E. Guhrauer, *Gottfried Wilhelm Freiherr von Leibniz—Eine Biographie,* 2 vols. Breslau: F. Hirt, 1842.

The only biographies in English are two older works:

J. M. Mackie, *Life of G. W. Leibniz.* Boston: Gould, Kendall, & Lincoln, 1845.

John Theodore Merz, *Leibniz.* Edinburgh and London: W. Blackwood & Sons, 1884.

Two works useful for setting the background against which the culture of Leibniz' place and time is to be understood are:

P. Hazard, *The European Mind: 1680-1715.* Engl. tr., J. Lewis. London: Hollis & Carter, 1953.

R. W. Meyer, *Leibniz and the Seventeenth-Century Revolution.* Engl. tr., J. P. Stern. Chicago: Henry Regnery Co., 1952.

one

GOD AND THE MIND OF GOD

God

Leibniz, more than any other modern philosopher, took seriously the idea of a *creation* of the universe, giving it a centrally important place in his system. Like the theories of the medievals for whom he had such great respect, his system put God as the *author of creation* at the focal position in metaphysics. The concept of God provides the theoretical foundation upon which the structure of the Leibniz metaphysic is built.

God, for Leibniz, may be defined as "the perfect being." [1] His existence is not a seriously problematic issue; it follows directly from the idea (or essence) of his perfection, by reasonings along the lines of the Ontological Argument of Anselm as refurbished by Descartes, and also by other, related arguments—a topic to which we will return at some length. Indeed, all characteristics of God must inhere in and derive from His attribute as "the perfect being." Three of these characteristics are of primary importance for Leibniz:

---

[1] *Un estre absolument parfait. Phil.*, IV, p. 427.

11

omniscience, omnipotence, and (omni–) benevolence.[2] These are the operative theological concepts in terms of which the drama of creation unfolds itself.

Substance

In the philosophy of Leibniz, as in that of Descartes and Spinoza, the conception of *substance* plays a fundamental role. Leibniz defines a substance as "a being capable of action." [3] God, of course, is a substance—the primordial substance, the only substance that exists in its own right. All other substances are in the first instance mere possibilities whose actualization hinges upon God, upon the creation. The prime characteristics of Leibniz' *substance* are: 1) a given individual substance is a simple, perduring existent, not in the sense of logical simplicity, but in the absence of spatial parts; 2) a given individual substance is capable of functioning as the subject of propositions, the predicates of true propositions concerning the substance standing for attributes of the substance. One can loosely describe Leibniz' individual substance as a spatio-temporal existent (God apart) without spatial parts, but not without attributes, and with a perduring individuality. One of Leibniz' own characterizations, helpful but incomplete unless interpreted in the context of many variant characterizations, reads as follows:

> There are only *atoms of substance,* that is to say, real unities, that are absolutely devoid of parts, which are the sources of action and the absolute first principles of the composition of all things and, as it were, are the ultimate elements in the analysis of substantial things. One could call them *metaphysical points.* They have something vital, a kind of perception; and mathematical points are their *points of view,* from which they express the universe.[4]

In a cognate passage we read that the individual substances, the monads,

---

[2] This is explicit in, e.g., the essay *Causa Dei asserta per justitiam ejus cum caeteris ejus perfectionibus. Phil.,* VI, pp. 437 ff. Leibniz follows in the footsteps of the tradition of those who, like St. Thomas Aquinas, hold God to be perfect in being, knowledge, and wisdom. Cf. *Monadology,* §4.

[3] "Principles of Nature and of Grace," §1. (This work is henceforth cited as PNG.)

[4] *Phil.,* IV, pp. 482-83.

cannot have shapes, otherwise they would have parts. And consequently a monad, in itself, and at a given moment, cannot be distinguished from another except by its internal qualities and actions
which cannot be otherwise than its *perceptions* (i.e., representations
of the compound, or of what is outside, in the simple) and its appetitions (i.e., its tendencies to pass from one perception to another),
which are the principles of change. . . . It [viz. a monad] is as a
center or a point where, simple though it is, an infinity of angles
are found made by the lines that come together there.[5]

The identification of the simple (primitive) predicates entering into
the defining notions of substances with the simple perfections of
God is a point repeatedly insisted upon by Leibniz.[6] This aspect of
substances draws together several strands of thought in Leibniz'
system, such as his thesis of the varying degrees of perfection (and
correlatively their imperfection or finitude), and his penchant for
the Ontological Argument for the existence of God. Moreover, it accounts for his conception of the immanence of God in monadic
life, a conception which led some writers to class Leibniz among
the medieval and Renaissance mystics in whose ideas he displayed
great interest.

Against the Cartesian notion of physical substance as pure extension, Leibniz cast three objections of a fundamentally conceptual
character: extension cannot comprise the essence of material substance because 1) it is an *incomplete* notion; 2) it is a *complex* and
not a simple concept, since it can be analyzed further into plurality,
continuity, and coexistence; [7] 3) the very conception of extension
is in its genesis imaginary and phenomenal, since size, figure, and
so on, are not distinct self-subsisting things, but are relative to our
perceptions.[8]

Substance *Sub Ratione Possibilitatis*

Prior to the creation [9] (and we think here not of literal and temporal but of figurative and conceptual priority) all substances aside

---

5 *Phil.*, VI, p. 598; PNG, §2.
6 See, for example, *Phil.*, V, p. 15 (bottom).
7 *Phil.*, II, pp. 169-70.
8 *Discourse on Metaphysics*, §xii. (This essay is henceforth cited as DM.)
9 *Phil.*, VI, p. 614.

from God existed, or rather *subsisted*—since *ex hypothesi* they did not exist—only as ideas in the mind of God:

> in God is found not only the source of existence, but also that of essences, insofar as they are real. In other words, He is the ground of what is real in the possible. For the Understanding of God is the region of the eternal truths and of the ideas on which they depend; and without Him there would be nothing real in the possibilities of things, and not only would there be nothing in existence, but nothing would even be possible.[10]

It should be stressed, however, that although presence in God's thoughts gives to unexistent possibles whatever "existence" they possess, the *nature* of such possibilities is wholly self-determined and in no way subject to God's will.

Since God is omniscient, His concept of the substance is not approximate and incomplete but descends to every detail of its (possible) career, and includes every single one of its properties. With respect to possibles, the principle obtains that alternative "descriptions" of the same thing must, unlike actual existents, be *logically* equivalent. In God's plan for ontological possibilities there is no room for the sort of incompleteness that figures in recipes for cooking or plans of architects ("Take 1 pint of milk." But from which cow? "Use such-and-such a piece of lumber." But from which tree?). Thus every possible substance, not only the ones actually singled out for creation, is represented in the mind of God by what Leibniz calls its *complete individual notion (notio completa seu perfecta substantiae singularis),* in which every detail of the substance at every stage of its (potential) career is fixed.[11] For simplicity and convenience we shall call this complete individual notion of the (possible) substance its *program.* The history of a substance is merely the continuous unfolding of its program with the same inexorable inevitability with which a mathematical series is generated in the successive development of its defining law. This lawfulness comprises the essence of the substance and is the source of its continuing self-identity: "That there is a certain persisting law

---

10 To speak of anything "prior" to the existent universe is to use the term in a purely logical, and by no means temporal, sense; and when one does so, one deals with the necessary being, the necessary truths, and the possible worlds, i.e., one enters the sphere of pure logic. It is hardly possible to find here a place for activity of any sort.

11 *Monadology,* §43.

which involves the future states of that which we conceive as the same—this itself is what I say constitutes the same substance." [12] In view of its specifications through its complete individual notion, every substance "contains in its nature a *law of the continuation of the series* of its own operations and [thus] of everything that has happened or will happen to it." [13] The complete individual notion of a substance is, of course, known only to God, not to mortals:

> The notion of myself, and of any other individual substance, is infinitely more extensive and more difficult to understand than is a generic concept like that of a sphere, which is only incomplete. . . . Therefore, although it is easy to determine that the number of feet in the diameter is not involved in the concept of a sphere in general, it is not so easy to decide if the journey which I intend to make is involved in my notion; otherwise it would be as easy for us to become prophets as to be Geometers.[14]

The contemplation of substances—not as existent actualities but as subsistent possibilities—forms in God's mind a "realm of possibles" (*pays des possibles*) in which every conceivable substance is presented "under the aspect of possibility" (*sub ratione possibilitatis*).[15] In God's mind we find the entire gamut of cosmological possibilities. (Note here the echo of Nicholas of Cusa's idea of the world as *explicatio dei,* its history being the unfolding of the divine plan, the "reading off" in nature of the book of God.) This part of the contents of the divine mind, the possible worlds, we must study, for it is an essential preliminary to a discussion of Leibniz' theory of creation.

Any actual state of affairs could, conceivably, have been different, for such an assumption involves no contradictory consequences. But if any actual state of affairs were different, then, since it is but the outcome of a natural course of development,[16] the entire universe would have to have a different history of development. In fact, we should have to resort to a world different from ours, involving another possible development of things: our hypothetical investigation would lead us to another, altogether different possible

12 *Phil.,* II, p. 264.
13 *Phil.,* IV, pp. 432-33; Couturat, *Opuscules,* pp. 403, 520.
14 *Phil.,* II, p. 45.
15 This is the key idea of one of Leibniz' ways of establishing the existence of God, since not even possibles would exist without the existence of "a being who could produce the possible" (*Phil.,* III, p. 572).
16 In Leibniz, one must remember, we are confronted with a strict mechanist.

world. Anterior to the existence of our world there was recorded in the divine mind entire infinities of notions of possible individual substances, whose only being at this point is that *sub ratione possibilitatis* in God's mind.

Compossibility and Order

Since the program of a substance involves the specification of literally every facet of its career, it involves all details of the relation of this substance to others. But now suppose that:

1. Possible substance #1 has the property P and also has the property that there is no substance having property Q to which it (#1) stands in the relationship R.
2. Possible substance #2 has the property Q and also has the property that every substance having the property P stands in the relationship R to it (#2).

These two substances are patently incompatible (on logical grounds). God might realize #1 or He might realize #2, but He cannot possibly realize both of them. (It is a fundamental tenet of Leibniz' philosophy that even omnipotence cannot accomplish the impossible.) Substances which do *not* clash in this way are characterized by Leibniz as *compossible*.

Thus the very concept (i.e., the defining program) of a possible substance marks it as either compossible or incompossible with any other given substance, and the fact that a given substance is compossible with such and such others must be incorporated in its concept. Since each of these possible substances involves one possible history of the development of the universe, only those involving the same history are compatible with each other. Because the actualization of some possibilities is incompatible with that of others, the manifold of possible substances splits into mutually exclusive systems of "compossibles." God's choice of creation is not of selection among individual substances, but among entire possible worlds; His will thus being always general "God never has a *particular will.*" [17]

---

17 *Theodicy*, §206.

Possible Worlds

There is an important difference between the *compossibility* of (possible) substances and the *compatibility* of propositions. One proposition can be mutually compatible with each of two others which are, in turn, incompatible with one another. This can happen only when the first proposition is "incomplete," i.e., simply fails to embody any information that commits it one way or another as regards the other two incompatible ones. Since this sort of incompleteness is excluded from the realm of the "complete individual concepts" of possible substances, it follows that whenever one substance is compossible with each of two others, they in turn must be compossible with one another. This is a consequence of the descriptive *completeness* with which every possible substance is identified in terms of its complete individual notion.

By means of this principle the possible substances sort themselves out into *possible worlds*. The possible world of any substance is the totality of all substances compossible with it. Each possible world consists of a family of possible substances, every one of which is compossible with all the rest, and the individual characteristics (and therefore, as we shall see, the mutual relations) of which are determined in every conceivable respect by their individual defining concepts. The substances of each possible world are thus reciprocally adjusted to one another in a thoroughgoing, *total* way. To use one of Leibniz' favorite metaphors, the substances of a possible world "mirror" one another in their mutual accommodation.[18] Since the entire history of each possible world is determined in every possible detail in terms of the complete individual notions of its constituent substances, there is no question of God's direct, immediate intervention in the course of natural events. (The possibility of divine action *within* the course of history is denied by Leibniz, so he rejects on this score both occasionalism and the interventionalism of Newton's divine clock-readjustor. Leibniz does, in the *Theodicy,* admit the possibility of continuous "creation," but this is not a matter of the introduction of new substances but of the

---

[18] It is derived from Nicholas of Cusa, according to whom the entire universe is a mirror of God.

temporal *continuation* of existing ones in accordance with a pre-established program.) [19]

Creation and the Actual World

If the concept of creation is to be introduced into the ontological framework just outlined in a viable way, the question of the existence of a possible substance must not be pre-empted by its complete individual notion. Thus Leibniz must either 1) adopt (i.e., anticipate) the Kantian course of denying that existence is a predicate, or else, 2) granting that existence is a predicate, rule existence out from the sphere of predicates that can feasibly enter into the defining notion of individual substances. Although in view of the paucity of evidence one cannot speak very firmly, it does appear that Leibniz took the second course, being willing to regard existence as a predicate,[20] albeit one of a sort that cannot enter into the essence of a substance (other than God), being inevitably consequent upon a pre-specified essence.[21]

The question can be raised: Is there anything to a Leibnizian substance over and above the attributes that belong to it by virtue of the predicates loaded into its complete individual notion? From the human standpoint the answer is *yes*—we actually do not ever know the complete individual notion of a substance, but encounter that substance only in experience (in fact, in confused perception). Even from God's standpoint an affirmative answer must be given, for an existing substance is, *ex hypothesi,* or *existent,* i.e., an entity or a thing, and its existence is never a matter of the attributes overtly guaranteed by its complete individual notion.

Suppose that God, contemplating a conceivable world *sub ratione possibilitatis,* finds it meritorious and chooses to *create* it, i.e., advance it from the status of a *possible* to that of an *actual* substance. Since He is omniscient, He knows the relationship of this substance to all the others that are compossible or incompossible with it.

---

[19] Cf. DM, §xxx: "God in co-operating with our actions ordinarily does no more than to follow the laws He has established, which is to say that He continually preserves and produces our being in such a way that thoughts come to us spontaneously or freely in the order carried in the concept of our individual substance, in which it could have been foreseen through all eternity."

[20] *Phil.,* V, p. 339. Cf. Russell, *Critical Exposition,* pp. 77, 174, 185.

[21] *Phil.,* VII, p. 195.

Being beneficent He wishes to *maximize existence,* to create as much as possible,[22] and thus would not choose to actualize a certain possible substance without actualizing other substances compossible with it—i.e., its entire possible world. But which of the possible worlds is God to choose for actualization? Clearly, the answer must be *the best.*[23] But what criterion of merit does God employ to determine whether one possible world is more or less perfect than another?

The Criterion of Goodness

The criterion of goodness for possible worlds is plainly set forth by Leibniz in the following terms:

> God has chosen [to create] that world which is the most perfect, that is to say, which is at the same time the simplest in its hypotheses [i.e., its laws] and the richest in phenomena.[24]

The characteristic properties of each substance change from one juncture to another in accordance with its program. The properties of substance #1 at one juncture may be more or less in accordance with and thus reflected or mirrored in those of substance #2 at this juncture. Out of these mirroring relationships grow the regularities which represent the "hypotheses," the natural laws of the possible worlds. The "best," most perfect possible world is that which exhibits the greatest *variety of its contents* (richness of phenomena) consonant with the greatest *simplicity of its laws.*

Our world—the actual world—is the "best possible world" in this rarified metaphysical sense of *greatest variety of phenomena consonant with greatest simplicity of laws.* Its being the best has (at bottom) little to do with how men (or men and animals) fare in it. The facile optimism of Dr. Pangloss, the butt of Voltaire's parody *Candide—Si c'est ici le meilleur des mondes possibles, que sont donc les autres?* [25]—misses the mark if Leibniz (and not some naive and simple-minded Leibnizian) is intended as its target.

There is, to be sure, a genuine difficulty in the Leibnizian criterion of which he himself was unquestionably aware, but which he did

---

22 Leibniz is fundamentally committed to the idea that existence is preferable to nonexistence.
23 We return to the topic of creation at greater length in Sec. 4 of Chap. 5.
24 DM, §6. Cf. *ibid.,* §5, and also PNG, §10; *Theodicy,* §208.
25 Voltaire, *Candide,* Chap. vi.

not resolve with the sharpness we might wish for. If merit of a possible world is determined by macro-considerations that operate in the large ("variety," "simplicity"), what assurance is there that the outcome is as we would wish it to be on the basis of micro-considerations that operate in the small (specifically, enumeration of the individual perfections of the several substances that comprise the possible worlds)? Leibniz adduces considerations which may mitigate, but do not wholly remove, doubt:

> The ways of God are those most simple and uniform . . . [being] the most productive in relation to the *simplicity of ways and means.* It is as if one said that a certain house was the best that could have been constructed at the same cost. . . . If the effect were assumed to be greater, but the process less simple, I think one might say when all is said and done, that the effect itself would be less great, taking into account not only the final effect but also the mediate effect. For the wisest mind so acts, as far as is possible, that the *means* are also *ends* of a sort, i.e., are desirable not only on account of what they do, but on account of what they are.[26]

This line of approach glosses over the genuine difficulty of a possibility of conflict between the components of Leibniz' two-factor criterion: What is to be chosen when we confront, for example, a sacrifice in "simplicity of means" for the sake of a greater "variety of phenomena"?

The Monads and God

An existing substance that is a member of the actual, and thus of the best possible, world, Leibniz calls a *monad.* He did not introduce the term monad until relatively late in his career. In the *Discourse on Metaphysics* of 1685, the first systematic presentation of his doctrine, he spoke simply of "individual substances." He continued to use this term, sometimes alternating it with *substantial form* and *entelechy,* or (when appropriate in context) *soul* or *spirit.* The term monad first began to be generally used by Leibniz in

---

26 *Theodicy,* §208.
27 See A. G. Langley (tr.), *G. W. Leibniz: New Essays Concerning Human Understanding* (New York & London: Macmillan Co., 1896), p. 101, notes. Cf. also Gerhardt's observations in *Phil.,* IV, pp. 417-18. Prof. L. E. Loemker informs me, however, that Leibniz employed the term *monas* (pl. *monades*)—albeit in a mathematical sense—as early as the Leipzig period.

1696.[27] Little else can be said about this definition apart from a question that has created something of a flurry of controversy among Leibniz scholars: Is God Himself a monad?

The answer to this must be in the affirmative. God is a monad, but a very special and unique one, for he is the *supreme* and the *prime* monad. The idea that God is a monad was called into question by Bertrand Russell,[28] who proposed to regard those passages where Leibniz explicitly speaks of God as one among the monads [29] as mere "slips." I think it unfortunate to charge an author with more mistakes than absolutely necessary, and see no reason why we must view Leibniz' declarations that God is a monad as errors from the standpoint of his system. That His status is fundamentally similar to that of the monads can be seen from the fact that He, like them, is an existing substance, indeed the supreme substance.[30] Leibniz explicitly assigns God a place in the scale of monads, holding Him to be the highest spirit.[31] Moreover, if God were not a monad it would be a contrastless qualification and senseless redundancy for Leibniz to speak, as he does often, of *created* substances and *created* monads, since God is the only noncreated existent in his ontology. In summary, we may regard it as certain that God has a place in Leibniz' system of monads, although this place is beyond any question a special and pre-eminent one.

---

[28] Russell, *Critical Exposition*, p. 187.
[29] For example, *Phil.*, III, p. 636; *Phil.*, VIII, p. 502.
[30] *Monadology*, §40.
[31] *Phil.*, IV, p. 460.

two

THREE FUNDAMENTAL
PRINCIPLES

Subject-Predicate Logic

Since the books of Russell and Couturat were published in the first decade of this century, it has become a generally emphasized thesis that Leibniz is fundamentally committed to a subject-predicate logic. The orthodox subject-predicate logician holds that every (meaningful) proposition is of the subject-predicate form, or somewhat less stringently, a proposition need not be exactly of this form but then must be a complex proposition that can be obtained by combining strictly subject-predicate propositions with syncategorematic connectives. It must be said emphatically that Leibniz is not, strictly speaking, a subject-predicate logician in this sense of the term, for he does not hold the position in full generality—with respect to propositions of all logical types—but *only with respect to propositions about substances,* i.e., about existents or possible existents. His version of the subject-predicate thesis is not a logical one regarding the general nature of propositions,[1] but a specifically metaphysical one about the nature of existents.

The Nature of "Analysis"

The Leibnizian "analysis" of a proposition about a substance consists of two steps:

1. To scrutinize the list of properties of the substance that is the subject of the proposition in order to determine what is and what is not included in its complete individual notion.
2. To determine whether the properties imputed by the predicate of the proposition to the substance are in fact included in this list (or is a derivative of properties so included).

If possession of the properties P and Q were included in the complete individual notion of substance #323, this fact would underwrite the analyticity of each of the following propositions:

"Substance #323 has the property P"
"Substance #323 has the property P-and-Q"
"Substance #323 has the property P-or-R"

It is important to recognize that Leibnizian "analysis" is a logical process of a very rudimentary sort, based on the inferential procedures of *definitional replacement* and *determination of predicational containment* through explicit use of logical processes of inference. This process is more complicated than Kant's mode of "analysis," which envisages only the presence of *explicit* predicational containments after definitional replacements have been carried out.

When more than a single substance is involved—perhaps in a relational proposition about two substances—the process is much the same, but on an extended scale. Thus the "analysis" of the proposition "Substance s_1 has the same color as substance s_2" would proceed as follows:

---

[1] To say this is not to deny that Leibniz thought the logical power of the subject-predicate form to be generally underrated. For example, he applied the subject-predicate formula not only to the four forms of categorical propositions, but to hypothetical propositions as well.

1. The complete individual notion of substance s_1 includes the color predicate C.

2. The complete individual notion of substance s_2 includes the color predicate C.

3. Whenever substance x has the color predicate X and substance y has the color predicate Y, and $X = Y$, then substance x has the same color as substance y.

Each of these is true "by definition," the first with reference to the complete individual notions of particular substances, the third a general definition of the concept "has the same color as," and on the basis of these the proposition in question can be derived by logical manipulations alone, using definitions to eliminate defined terms. This procedure characterizes the analysis of propositions. As this sketch (rightly) suggests, Leibniz agrees entirely with Hobbes' view that only definitions are primary truths.[2]

One further complication must be introduced. In the case of certain, especially complex, propositions this process of analysis may be nonterminating (i.e., infinite). In the previous examples the analysis resulted in an explicit identity after a finite number of steps, but such a brief termination need not necessarily be the case, according to Leibniz. Analysis of certain propositions will not result in *explicit* identities; they are only *virtually* identical, in that their analysis comes closer and closer to yielding, but never actually yields, an actual identity. There can be no doubt that Leibniz' views on this, however greatly indebted to his work on the infinitesimal calculus, were influenced by the teaching of Nicholas of Cusa (in Chaps. i-ii of *De docta ignorantia*) that truly accurate reasoning about matters of fact would require an infinite number of inferential steps between the premises and the ultimately desired conclusion, so that the human intellect can only approach, but never attain, the ultimate precision of truth (*praecisio veritatis*).[3]

---

2 Leibniz, however, departs from Hobbes with respect to the converse view that all definitions are truths, on the ground that definitions may involve contradictions, since "notions taken at random cannot always be reconciled among themselves" (*Phil.*, V, p. 425).

3 Nicholas even gives the mathematical analogue of the increasingly many-sided regular polygons inscribed in a circle whose content comes closer and closer to that of the circular disk in question without ever reaching it.

The Principle of Sufficient Reason
(Every True Proposition Is Analytic)

In Leibniz' conception, the characteristic that marks a proposition (of the subject-predicate form) as *true* is if that predicate is included in the list of characteristics comprising the definition—and, in the case of a substance, the complete individual notion—of the subject, i.e., that "the predicate is in the subject" (*praedicatium inest subjecto*). This conception of truth provides the basis for what Leibniz calls the *Principle of Sufficient Reason,* a principle basic to his entire philosophical system. Opposing the view that truth is a matter of arbitrary human conventions, as with Hobbes, or that truth is grounded in the arbitrary will of God, as with Descartes, Leibniz maintains that the truth and falsity of propositions invariably have a non-arbitrary grounding in "the nature of things." This is codified in his Principle of Sufficient Reason. According to the principle, *every true proposition is analytic.* As explained in the previous section, a proposition is analytic if a process of "analysis," substitutions for defined terms of their definitions, can reduce the proposition to an overt identity, a logical truth. The principle in question thus maintains that every true proposition is either finitely or infinitely analytic; its analysis either results in an explicit identity or the identity is only a virtual one that can be reached after any finite number of steps, but only "in the limit."

The analysis at issue here may, and generally will, be one which God alone can carry out, whereas we mere mortals cannot. In one place Leibniz puts the matter as follows:

> In contingent truths, however, though the predicate inheres in the subject, we can never demonstrate this, nor can the proposition ever be reduced to an equation or an identity, but the analysis proceeds to infinity, only God being able to see, not the end of the analysis indeed, since there is no end, but the nexus of terms, or the inclusion of the predicate in the subject, since he sees everything which is in the series.[4]

---

4 *Philosophical Papers and Letters* (ed. Loemker), p. 407.

Unlike men, God can carry out this analysis because His processes of reasoning are not only of greater scope than ours, but also vastly more efficient: He can deal with concepts and truths *directly*, whereas for us such dealings must be indirect, by words and sentences.[5]

The Principle of Identity (or of Contradiction) (Every Finitely Analytic Proposition Is True, Indeed Necessarily True)

The converse of the Principle of Sufficient Reason would of course read *every finitely or infinitely analytic proposition is true.* This results in a pair of theses, to wit, *every finitely analytic proposition is true* and *every infinitely analytic proposition is true.* Postponing for the moment the issue of infinitely analytic propositions, let us focus upon the first of these principles, to the effect that all finitely analytic propositions represent truths. This thesis is Leibniz' *Principle of Contradiction.*

A finitely analytic proposition, it will be recalled, is one that is either explicitly identical ("An equilateral rectangle is a rectangle" is a favorite example) or one that can be reduced to an explicitly identical proposition by a finite number of steps of reasoning using definitions alone. Since this process of analysis is such as to exhibit that (and how) the predicate of the proposition is contained in the defining concept of its subject, it is clear that such a finitely analytic proposition will not only be true, but *necessarily* true. The *Principle of Identity* is thus the governing principle for the domain of necessary truths.

When a proposition falls under the Principle of Identity, its denial would not only be false, but contradictory of itself, since it denies that the predicate belongs to the subject when the analysis in question shows that it does demonstrably so belong. From this standpoint, the Principle of Identity can also be regarded from the negative angle as the Principle of Contradiction. Leibniz frequently speaks of the matter in this way, and refers to the principle of the

---

[5] These themes are pursued at some length in the *New Essays;* see especially Bk. III.

necessary truths—that all finitely analytic propositions are necessary truths—as the Principle of Contradiction. It is clear, however,
that he envisages but a single principle, two alternative versions of
which are at issue.

The Principle of Perfection (or of the Best)
(Every Infinitely Analytic Proposition Is
True, i.e., Contingently True)

When a proposition is infinitely analytic, its predicate cannot be
shown to inhere in its subject by any finite process of demonstration
—it is not an "actually identical" proposition, but is only "virtually
identical," the identity being one that can be shown to obtain only
"in the limit." But exactly how are we to conceive of such an
infinite process of analysis that exhibits the "virtually identical" of
an infinitely analytic proposition?

Every possible substance is a member of some possible world, and
its complete notion involves its entire history in the development
of that possible universe.[6] To every state in the development of a
possible substance there corresponds a state of every other possible
substance of its possible world, a correspondence capable of varying
degrees of closeness of agreement between its members. Thus within
a possible world every substance "represents" every other substance
more or less "distinctly," or, inversely, it "perceives" the other substance with a greater or lesser degree of "clarity" or "confusion."
In this way, at each stage of its development every possible substance "perceives" or "mirrors" its entire universe, and moreover
does so more or less clearly as the mean value of the degree of
clarity of its perception of individual substances varies. Let us call
the degree of clarity with which at a given state a possible substance
mirrors its universe its *amount of perfection for that state*. Now
what Leibniz terms the amount of perfection of a possible substance

---

6 Leibniz claims that this is a logical consequence of the Principle of Sufficient
Reason. The deduction he offers, along with a commentary, is given in Couturat's article, "La métaphysique de Leibniz" in *Revue de Métaphysique et
de Morale*, vol. 10 (1902). See also the suggestive discussion by C. D. Broad,
"Leibniz' Predicate-in-Notion Principle and Some of Its Alleged Consequences," *Theoria*, vol. 15 (1949), 54-70.

is a measure of its amount of perfection for *all* states.[7] Consequently every possible universe also has an amount of perfection, the sum total of the amounts of perfection of the possible substances belonging to it.

In His selection of one among the possible worlds for actualization, God subscribes to a certain determinative principle. This is the *Principle of Perfection or of the Best*.[8] In accord with this principle God selects that universe for which the amount of perfection is a maximum.[9] This principle is a formulation of the thesis that, in His decision of creation, God acted in the best possible way; the actual world is that one among the possible worlds which an infinite process of comparison showed to be the best.

The existence of an objective criterion of goodness for possible worlds wholly independent of the will of God is a crucial feature of this principle. And Leibniz emphatically maintains that:

> In saying, therefore, that things are not good according to any standard of goodness, but simply by the will of God, it seems to me that one destroys, without realizing it, all the love of God and all His glory; for why praise Him for what he has done, if he would be equally praiseworthy in doing the contrary? . . . This is why, accordingly, I find so strange those expressions of certain philosophers who say that the eternal truths of metaphysics and geometry, and so also the principles of goodness, of justice, and of perfection, are effects only of the will of God.[10]

---

[7] This theory of perception and its relation to perfection is presented in barest outline in Sections 14 and 49 of the *Monadology*. The following references prove especially illuminating as regards Leibniz' concept of perception: *Phil.*, I, pp. 383-84; VI, p. 604; VII, p. 529. On the relation of perfection to perception see also *Phil.*, II, p. 451.

[8] "Principe de la perfection," *"Lex melioris,"* "Principe du meilleur," "Principe de la convenance."

[9] This conception of the relation of perfection to existence makes it possible for Leibniz to identify the "quantity of essence" of a possible substance, which determines its potentiality for existence, with its amount of perfection. "Everything possible . . . tends with equal right towards existence according to its quantity of essence or reality, or to the degree of perfection which it involves, perfection being nothing but the quantity of essence" (*Phil.*, VII, p. 303). Since the more clearly a substance perceives another, the greater the compatibility of its own state with that perceived, perfection increases with compossibility. Thus, "just as possibility is the principle of essence, so perfection or the quantity of essence (which measures the number of compossibles of a thing) is the principle of existence" (*Phil.*, VII, p. 304). Hence the Principle of Perfection makes it possible for Leibniz to state that "one can define as existent that which is compatible with more things than anything incompatible with it" (Couturat, *Opuscules*, p. 360).

[10] DM, §2.

The Principle of Perfection is Leibniz' philosophic formulation of the theological principle of God's goodness. It asserts that in the creation of the world God acted in the best way possible. The principle is not a logical, but a fundamentally ethical one, akin in its character to the jurists' dictum: *Quae contra bones mores sunt ea nec facere nos posse credendum est*.[11] Leibniz bitterly opposed the position of Descartes and Spinoza, whom he took to maintain the indifference and arbitrariness of God's will. He was eager to combat any manifestation of the view:

> . . . the extremely dangerous [view], almost approaching that of re-
> cent innovators, whose opinion is that the beauty of the universe,
> and the goodness that we attribute to the works of God, are nothing
> more than the chimeras of men who conceive God after their own
> fashion. . . . [And who] also say that things are not good by any
> rule of goodness, but only by the will of God, one destroys, it seems
> to me, without realizing it, all love of God and all God's glory.[12]

That possible things are good objectively by a "règle de bonté" which is operative independently of the will of God, but that in His decisions of creation God freely subscribes to the valuations of this "règle de bonté" is the content of Leibniz' Principle of Perfection.

Leibniz repeatedly says that all possible substances have "a certain urge (*exigentia*) toward existence"; since to be a possible is to be a possibly *existing* thing, we find in possibles a *conatus,* a dynamic striving toward existence proportionate to the perfection of the substance. This way of talking has led certain commentators, primarily A. O. Lovejoy,[13] to argue that Leibniz' talk of the selection of a (i.e., the best) possible world for actualization by God is a pointless redundancy, since it is the intrinsic nature of these substances to prevail in the struggle for existence among alternative possibilities. But this approach misconceives the issue badly, for it is only because God *has chosen* to subscribe to the standard of perfection in selecting a possible world for actualization that possible substances come to have (figurative) "claim" to existence. The relationship

---

11 "The things that go against moral principles are also not to be thought possible actions for us" (*Phil.,* VII, p. 278).
12 *Phil.,* VI, p. 428.
13 A. O. Lovejoy, *The Great Chain of Being* (Cambridge, Mass.: Harvard University Press, 1936), p. 179.

between "quantity of essence" or "perfection" [14] on the one hand and claim or *conatus* to existence on the other is not a logical linkage at all—a thesis which would reduce Leibniz' system into a Spinozistic necessitarianism—but a connection mediated by a free act of will on the part of God.

In accord with the Principle of Perfection, the actual world as a whole is as perfect as possible; each of its parts is itself, in turn, as perfect as possible. There are not, as with Descartes, partial imperfections compensated for by the perfection of the whole. Each part of the world aids in the maximization of perfection by contributing the maximum of perfection that is, under the circumstances, possible for it.[15]

Thus the Principle of Perfection is a maximum principle, and it furnishes the mechanism of God's decision among the infinite, mutually exclusive systems of compossibles. It has as its immediate consequence that God actualized that possible world in which perfection is at a maximum. God is perfect, and consequently the only outlet for that perfection—the world—is perfect. Within the limits of possibility the actual world contains the most perfection, hence also the most existence.[16]

---

[14] "Perfection is nothing but the quantity of essence" (*Phil.*, VII, p. 303). The entire context of this passage in the essay "On the Radical Origin of Things" (*De rerum origionatione radicali; Phil.*, VII, pp. 302-8; Loemker, pp. 789-98) is crucially relevant to the present discussion.

[15] "The Principle of Perfection is not limited to the general but descends also to the particulars of things and of phenomena and that in this respect it closely resembles the method of optimal forms, that is to say, of forms which provide a maximum or minimum, as the case may be—a method which I have introduced into geometry in addition to the ancient method of maximal and minimal quantities. For in these forms or figures the optimum is found not only in the whole but also in each part, and it would not even suffice in the whole without this. . . ." And after citing as an example the remarkable properties of the cycloid, which we will later have occasion to consider, Leibniz continues: "It is in this way that the smallest parts of the universe are ruled in accordance with the order of greatest perfection . . ." (*Phil.*, VII, pp. 272-73).

[16] See *De rerum origionatione radicali* (1697), *Phil.*, VII, pp. 302 ff. Here is maintained "existere quantum plurimum protest pro temporis locique capacitate." By "essence" Leibniz understands potentiality for existence, thus quantity of essence varies directly as perfection. "All possible things, or things expressing an essence or possible reality, tend toward existence with equal right in proportion to the quantity of essence or reality, or to the degree of perfection which they involve; for perfection is nothing but quantity of essence" (*Phil.*, VII, p. 303). Cf. *Monadology*, §41: "Perfection being nothing but the magnitude

The Principle of Perfection resembles physical principles of a familiar kind. Leibniz himself makes much of such as the optical principles of least (or greatest, as the case may be) time and distance, and the principle of least action. The Principle of Perfection also specifies that in nature some quantity is at a maximum or a minimum, an idea which Leibniz often illustrates with the remark that in nature a drop of water will, if undisturbed, take on the form of a sphere, enclosing a maximal volume with a surface of given area. In other words, we have a "minimax" or "extremal" principle.[17] Like the others, it requires techniques analogous to those of the calculus, especially the calculus of variations. In fact, according to Leibniz' own statements, the principle was suggested to him by mathematical considerations.[18]

Perfection and Infinite Analysis

The Principle of Perfection enables us to understand what Leibniz intends when he speaks of the contingent truths as analytic, but requiring an infinite process for their analysis. A given proposition concerning a contingent existence is true, and its predicate is indeed contained in its subject, if the state of affairs characterized by this

---

of positive reality taken in its strictest sense. . . ." The actual world, therefore, having the maximum of perfection, contains the maximum of existence possible. Thus Leibniz gives the definition, "An *existent* is . . . [that] which is compatible with more things than are compatible with it" (Couturat, *Opuscules,* p. 360).

[17] See the *Tentamen Anagogicum* (*Phil.,* VII, pp. 270-79) on the minimax principles and their relation to the Principle of Perfection. The reader interested in Leibniz and the principle of least action is referred to the sixteenth note appended to Couturat's *Logique,* and to the Appendix to M. Gueroult's *Dynamique et métaphysique leibniziennes* (Paris: J. Vrin, 1934).

[18] "There is something which had me perplexed for a long time—how it is possible for the predicate of a proposition to be contained in (*inesse*) the subject without making the proposition necessary. But the knowledge of Geometrical matters, and especially of infinitesimal analysis, lit the lamp for me, so that I came to see that notions too can be resolvable *in infinitum*" (Couturat, *Opuscules,* p. 18). "At length some new and unexpected light appeared from a direction in which my hopes were smallest—from *mathematical* considerations regarding the nature of the infinite. In truth there are two labyrinths in the human mind, one concerning the composition of the continuum, the other concerning the nature of freedom. And both of these spring from exactly the same source—the infinite" (Couturat, *Logique,* p. 210, notes).

inclusion involves a greater amount of perfection for the world than any other possible state; i.e., if the state of affairs asserted by the proposition is one appropriate to the best possible world.

> All contingent propositions have sufficient reasons, or equivalently have a priori proofs which establish their certainty, and which show that the connection of subject and predicate of these propositions has its foundation in their nature. But it is not the case that contingent propositions have demonstrations of necessity, since their sufficient reasons are based on the principle of contingence or existence, i.e., on what seems best among the equally possible alternatives. . . .[19]

It is thus via the infinite comparison demanded by the Principle of Perfection that an infinite process is imported into the analysis of a truth dealing with contingent existence.

The Principle of Perfection is Leibniz' principle of contingence: it is in virtue of this principle that infinitely analytic propositions can be *truths.* Against the background of our exposition of Leibniz' conception of the infinite analyticity of the truths dealing with contingent existence, this should be clear. For it is due precisely to God's choice of the best of all possible worlds, and therefore to the Principle of Perfection, that those propositions dealing with the best possible universe deal with the actual one, and thus are true. It is indeed the Principle of Perfection which guarantees the truth of those propositions infinitely analytic in the sense discussed. Leibniz in one particularly revealing passage puts the matter as follows:

> But to say that God can only choose what is best, and to infer from thence that what He does not choose is impossible, this, I say, is a confounding of terms: 'tis blending power and will, metaphysical necessity and moral necessity, essences and existences. For what is [strictly or metaphysically] necessary is so by its essence, since its opposite implies a contradiction. But *a contingent which exists owes its existence to the principle of what is best (principe du meilleur), which is a sufficient reason for the existence of things.* And therefore I say that [morally necessitating] motives incline without necessitating [metaphysically]; and that there is a certainty and infallibility, but not an absolute necessity in contingent things.[20]

It is clear from the logic of the situation that the Principles of Sufficient Reason and of Contradiction require an additional prin-

---

19 *Phil.,* IV, pp. 438-39.
20 *Phil.,* VII, p. 390; 5th letter to Clarke, §9. Our italics.

ciple of contingence. The Principle of Perfection serves this function: "A contingent existent owes its existence to the Principle of Perfection, which is the sufficient reason for existents." [21] Leibniz calls the "necessity" of contingent truths *moral necessity* as opposed to the *logical* or *geometric* or *absolute* or *metaphysical necessity* of necessary truths, and he states that "moral necessity stems from the choice of the best." [22] In §46 of the *Monadology* Leibniz speaks of "the contingent truths whose principle is that of suitability or of the choice of the best." And he maintains that "contingent propositions have demonstrations . . . based on the principle of contingence or existence, i.e., on what seems best among the several equally possible alternatives. . . ." [23] Finally he contrasts "the necessary truths whose necessity is brute and geometric" with "the truths whose source lies in suitability and final causes." [24]

A Polemical Digression

The Principle of Perfection has been systematically misconceived by commentators. Couturat, for example, holds, as we have seen, that the pair of Principles constituted by Sufficient Reason and Contradiction is complete; consequently, he holds that the Principle of Perfection is subsidiary, and indeed a *consequence* of the Principle of Sufficient Reason. [25] Now this surely cannot be the case. The Principle of Sufficient Reason demands *definiteness;* it states that a contingent truth is susceptible of an analysis which, though infinite, *converges on something.* But such definiteness could have been gained equally well had God chosen the worst or the most mediocre of all possible worlds. The Principle of Sufficient Reason requires merely *that* a contingent truth be analytic; the Principle of Perfection shows *how* this is the case. As Leibniz repeatedly insists, the Principle of Sufficient Reason, being an a priori consequence of the nature of truth, leaves entirely open to God's choice a gamut of alternatives for possible creation, of which the best

---

21 *Ibid.,* p. 390.
22 *Ibid.,* p. 409.
23 *Phil.,* IV, pp. 438-39.
24 *Phil.,* III, p. 645.
25 Couturat, *Logique,* p. 224.

possible world is only one. Therefore, though it is true that the Principle of Sufficient Reason requires some complementary principle of definiteness, Leibniz would have been the first to deny that this *must* be the Principle of Perfection.

Most commentators, including Erdmann, Latta, Joseph, and Russell, maintain that the Principle of Sufficient Reason is the principle of contingence, somehow subsuming the Principle of Perfection under this principle. Erdmann indeed goes so far as to identify the Principles of Sufficient Reason and Perfection.[26] This again cannot be so, not only for the reasons given, but also if we call to mind the previous characterization of Leibniz' three basic principles. All true propositions are analytic, finitely or infinitely (Principle of Sufficient Reason); all finitely analytic propositions are true (Principle of Contradiction); all infinitely analytic propositions—and thus all propositions whose infinite analysis converges on some characteristic of the best of all possible worlds—are true (Principle of Perfection). This is Leibniz' technical formulation of the three principles, and it puts their logical independence beyond doubt.

---

[26] J. E. Erdmann, *Grundriss der Geschichte der Philosophie* (Berlin: W. Hertz, 1896), Vol. II, 227; R. Latta, *Leibniz: The Monadology, and Other Philosophical Writings* (Oxford: Oxford University Press, 1898), p. 67; H. W. B. Joseph, *Lectures on the Philosophy of Leibniz* (Oxford: Clarendon Press, 1949), p. 114; B. Russell, *A Critical Exposition of the Philosophy of Leibniz*, 2d ed. (London: Cambridge University Press, 1937), p. 25.

three

THE THEORY OF
CONTINGENCE

The Role of Contingence

The question of whether or not Leibniz' metaphysical system makes room for genuine contingence—avoiding a general collapse into universal necessitarianism of the Spinozistic type—is one of the heated issues in debates among Leibniz scholars. There is no question that Leibniz *wished* to find a place for contingence; time and again he made claims to have done so, and pointed to the rejection of contingence in the system of Spinoza as a cardinal defect in his philosophy. But numerous commentators, Russell prominent among them, have held this desideratum to be improper for Leibniz, leading him into logical incompatibilities with key tenets of his system.

This question of contingence is a crucial issue for Leibniz' metaphysic, and lies at the very heart of his philosophy, for there is one group of occurrences in nature whose contingency is a life and death matter for Leibniz: man's choices, decisions, and free actions. If contingence goes by the board in Leibniz' system, so does free will, thus sounding the deathknell to the project of reconciliation, which was a central motive for Leibniz' construction of a philosophic system he regarded as capable of meeting all the rational exigencies of the world-view of contemporary science on one hand and of Christian doctrine on the other.

The Nature of Contingence

Leibniz' explanation of how it comes about that contingent truths are analytic, the analysis being infinite, but convergent, falls into three parts. The first of these explanations is popular in character, but the remaining two are complementary technical arguments, drawn from the theory of knowledge and from metaphysics, respectively.

The first way Leibniz shows that an infinite process enters into the analysis of a contingent truth is based on the fact that a contingent existent, being located in space and time, expresses its relations to two infinities of cognate contingents—its contemporaries in space, and its predecessors and successors in time. Leibniz argues that in the analysis of any statement concerning the contingent which is an effort to account for it or some of its aspects, these infinitudes of relata represent conditions that must be taken into account.[1] Everything in the world is mutually involved with everything else. (The Greek dictum *sympnoia panta*—"all things conspire together"—was a favorite with Leibniz.) Since the analysis of a contingent truth must proceed over an infinity of related contingents it can never be achieved fully by man, although it can become more and more complete. This popular, non-technical explanation may be regarded as an heuristic introduction to the remaining two arguments.

The second, epistemological way in which Leibniz conceives of the necessity of an infinite analysis of truths of fact is based on his

---

[1] "Indeed, even if the reason (cause) of a prior state could always be rendered from the one prior to that: yet its reason could in turn be given without reaching a last reason (cause) in the series. But this progression has the locus of its reason (cause) in the infinite, which, in some manner of its own, outside the series, in God, was immediately perceivable from the beginning by the Author of things, on whom depend both prior and posterior things, rather than [its being] he who, reciprocally, depends on them. Therefore whatever truth is not incapable of analysis and cannot be demonstrated from its own reasons but receives its ultimate reason and certitude only from the divine mind is not necessary. And such are all which I call *truths of fact*. And this is the root source of contingency . . ." (*Phil.*, VII, p. 200).

view of the nature of empirical predicates. He holds that the predicate of a factual assertion regarding a substance (actual or possible) is never simple, but always complex in such a way as to admit of an infinite regress in its analysis. Suppose the truth of the proposition

1. Substance s_1 has the property P,

and suppose further that

2. Substance s_2 has the property P.

It follows from 1 and 2 that

3. Substance s_1 has the property of having the property P in common with substance s_2.

Although we have derived 3 from 1 and 2 there must be, in view of Leibniz' internalized theory of relations yet to be discussed (in Chapter Six), a pure (nonrelational) property P^* of s_1 such that the statement

4. Substance s_1 has the property P^*

is *equivalent* with 3, i.e., amounts to something of the form

5. Substance s_1 has P-in-common-with s_2.

Since any two substances have some properties in common,[2] and since all such property sharings will be such that full analysis of the shared property leads to an involvement of further properties[3] —on an analogy with the transition from the P of 1 to the P^* of 4—the analysis of a statement predicating a property of a substance leads to an infinite regress.

We come now to the third and most important way of explaining the need for infinitistic analysis of contingent truths on Leibnizian grounds. Since true contingent propositions concern contingent *existents* (with one important exception, as we shall see), the concatenation of subject and predicate asserted by them depends on the nature of existence.[4] In this way the principle of contingent

---

[2] "For my part I do not consider A and B, if they have no predicate in common, to be possibles" (*Phil.*, II, p. 233).

[3] Thus Leibniz holds that "Nor do I find any entirely absolute predicates in notions, that is, any which do not involve connexions with other predicates" (*Phil.*, II, p. 249).

[4] Leibniz, in criticizing Spinoza for failing to provide a definition of "contingence," wrote: "I use the term *contingent,* as do others, for that whose essence does not involve existence. In this sense, particular things are contingent according to Spinoza himself in prop. 24 [of Bk. I of the *Ethics*]" (*Phil.*, I, p. 148).

existence, the Principle of Perfection, enters into their analysis.[5] It is via this principle, and comparison of perfection of an infinite number of possible worlds involved in it, that an infinite process is imported into the analysis of contingent truths. The infinite analysis of a contingent truth is conceived of on an analogy with the infinitistic comparison problems of the calculus of variations. This branch of mathematics, which numbers Leibniz among its founders, handles problems such as selecting from among the infinite number of equiperimetric triangles that of maximum area or from among the infinite number of curves that of fastest descent. Correspondingly, under the auspices of the Principle of Perfection, the divine mind solves such problems as selecting that possible world with the maximum of perfection, or that possible Adam whose existence entails the greatest number of desirable consequences.[6] Thus the Principle of Perfection provides the explanation of, and the mechanism for, the infinite analysis of contingent truths. A given proposition of the contingent type is true, and its subject includes its predicate, if the state of affairs characterized by this inclusion allows of greater perfection for the world than any other state of affairs. A truth of fact is such that the state of affairs it asserts is one belonging to the best of all possible worlds, hence its analysis, which consists in showing that this is indeed so, requires an infinite process of comparison.

---

5 "All contingent propositions have sufficient reasons, or, equivalently, have a priori proofs which establish their certainty, and which show that the connection of subject and predicate of these propositions has its foundation in their nature. But it is not the case that contingent propositions have demonstrations of necessity, since their sufficient reasons are based on the principle of contingence or of the existence of things, i.e., on what is or seems the best among equally possible alternatives, while necessary truths are founded upon the principle of contradictions and [on that] of the possibility or impossibility of the essences themselves, without having regard in that respect on the free will of God or of creatures" (*Phil.*, IV, pp. 438-39).

6 "The true reason why this thing which is better than that exists is to be subsumed under the free decrees of the divine will, of which the primary one is the decision to do everything in the best possible way, as seems wisest. Therefore it is occasionally permitted that a more perfect be excluded in favor of a less perfect; nevertheless in the sum that way of creating the world is chosen which involves more reality or perfection, and God works on the model of the master Geometer who in problems brings forth the best construction. Therefore all beings, insofar as they are involved in the first Being, have, above and beyond bare possibility, a propensity toward existing in proportion to their goodness, and they exist by the will of God unless they are incompatible with more perfect [existence-candidates]" (*Phil.*, VII, pp. 309-10).

Contingent truths of fact about the world actually involve a double involution of infinite analysis. Consider God as making, "prior" to the creation, some sort of inventory of the possible worlds. At this juncture every feature of the to-be-actualized world (perhaps possible world 3756) is a necessary feature of that world, inherent in its defining concept. Descriptive propositions about this *qua* possible world 3756 are never contingent. But the situation is altogether different when we consider this world *qua* the actually existing world, for the grounding of the existence of the world rests on three propositions:

1. Possible world 3756 has such-and-such features, whereas the features of the other possible worlds are. . . .
2. In view of 1, possible world 3756 meets the comparative criterion *C* (maximum perfection, i.e., variety-consonant-with-order).
3. God adopts criterion *C* as His creation-selection criterion, i.e., chooses to act in the most perfect way.

It is graphically clear from this perspective that 1 involves only necessary propositions and 2 involves an infinite process of comparative analysis. The ultimate source of contingent truth is clearly 3, to which we shall return (see section beginning on page 43). This localization of contingence in 3 rather than 1 rids God of any responsibility for specific features of the actual world over which he exercises absolutely no control, and avoids any imputation of imposing necessities upon the world:

> Nor does the foreknowledge or preordination of God impose necessity even though it is also infallible. For God has seen things in an ideal series of possibles, such as they were to be, and among them man freely sinning. By seeing the existence of this series He did not change the nature of the thing, nor did He make what was contingent necessary.[7]

We thus see how the Principle of Perfection is central to Leibniz' cosmology. It provides the *ratio essendi* of the actual world, and derivatively it provides the *principium reddendae rationis* [8] of the contingent truths, furnishing the means for their analysis. The fact that the Principle of Perfection is a maximum principle, conceived

---

[7] *Causa Dei,* prop. 104.

[8] For this expression, which is another name of the principle of sufficient reason, see *Phil.,* VII, p. 309; Couturat, *Opuscules,* p. 528; and also Couturat, *Logique,* p. 214, n. 2.

of on an analogy with the calculus of variations, is the reason why the analysis of truths of fact is infinite.

The Machinery of Analysis

The remark is due to Hero, and is also to be found in the Ptolemaic corpus, that in traveling from one point to another via a plane mirror a ray of light takes the shortest path.[9] In Leibniz' day a generalized version of this principle was beginning to find a place in optics. In about 1628 Fermat had developed a principle of least time which, together with a method of maxima and minima which anticipated the calculus, he used to deduce the laws of reflection and the newly discovered law of refraction.[10] Leibniz ardently espoused this principle, and reproached Descartes with having used, in accordance with the Cartesian program, a more clumsy mechanical method in the derivation of Snell's law of refraction, instead of the more elegant and fundamental principle of least time or distance.[11]

The mathematical problem of maxima and minima led Leibniz to extend Fermat's investigations, and resulted in invention of the differential calculus, but this does not concern us here. However, the optical minimum principle of least time also absorbed much of Leibniz' time and interest, and he generalized it in an important way.

This generalization of Fermat's principle of least time (or, equivalently in the case of a constant speed, of least distance) is to the effect that there need not be, in the usual transmission phenomena, a *minimization* of time. As Leibniz rightly points out, there might be a maximization, for example, in the case of a concave mirror.[12] But this does not undermine the general principle, for Leibniz remarks that the mathematical method for finding maxima and

9 See E. Mach, *Science of Mechanics*, tr. by P. E. B. Jourdain (La Salle, Ill.: Open Court Publishing Co., 1915), p. 518, and *Phil.*, VII, p. 274. Hero flourished around A.D. 100 and Ptolemy around A.D. 130.

10 The law of refraction is due to Snell, 1621, on whom see W. Whewell, *History of the Inductive Sciences* (London: J. W. Parker, 1840), II, p. 56, as well as *Phil.*, VII, pp. 273-78.

11 *Phil.*, VII, p. 274.

12 *Ibid.*, pp. 274-75.

minima which he developed—finding a zero of the first derivative—yields both maxima and minima without discriminating between them.[13]

Inspired by its success in optics, Leibniz sought ardently to extend the applicability of minimax principles by means of a general principle that in all natural processes some physical quantity is at a maximum or a minimum. He felt he had found a principle which cuts across the particular laws of physics, and clearly demonstrates the general interconnection of things. Here was a powerful unifying rule for the multitude of particular natural laws, giving coherence to natural science and showing clearly the economy in nature. He could draw upon pure mathematics, mechanics, optics, and dynamics for illustration of his principle.[14] It makes possible the deduction of a multitude of *ad hoc* laws from a simple general rule, and gives some insight into that remarkable unity of the phenomena on which Leibniz dwelt so fondly.[15] I will discuss only two of the examples which Leibniz regarded as illustrative of the unifying power revealed by this principle.

When one applies the rule of least time to obtain the law of refraction for a ray of light moving in the indicated direction from medium 1 to medium 2, with velocity $v(1)$ in medium 1 and $v(2)$ in medium 2, and with angle of incidence $A(1)$ and angle of refraction $A(2)$, one obtains the law: $v(1) : \sin A(1) :: v(2) : \sin A(2)$. But the law of reflection due to Hero (law of least distance, angle of incidence = angle of reflection is merely a special case of this law, for in reflection the ray remains in the same medium, hence its velocity remains the same.[16]

Another instance of the "conspiration universelle" revealed in the application of the minimax principle is given by the solution to the Brachistochrone problem. This problem is to find a curve, the Brachistochrone, which has the following property:

Suppose that two points in a vertical plane, A and B are given, A being the higher, and B located somewhere on the plane below. Let us imagine a particle starting from rest at A and rolling along a frictionless curved incline to B under the force of gravity (and a normal

13 *Ibid.*, p. 275.
14 See *passim* in the *Tentamen Anagogicum, Phil.*, VII, pp. 270-79.
15 He termed it "la conspiration universelle." The Hippocratean dictum "sympnoia panta" (all things conspire together) was a favorite with Leibniz.
16 See the *Randbemerkung, Phil.*, VII, p. 277; and see Mach, *op. cit.*, p. 521.

force exerted by the incline). The required curve is that one such that if the incline is installed along it the particle will accomplish its journey from A to B in the shortest time.[17]

It is necessary to determine "si ex datis pluribus infinitive quantitatibus invenienda sit una maxima vel minima," as John Bernouilli put it.[18] This curve of fastest descent, attainable by the mathematicals of the calculus, is the cycloid, the curve generated by the motion of a point on the circumference of a wheel rolling along a straight line. This curve has another remarkable property: "If in the case of the curve of shortest descent between two given points, we choose any two points on this curve at will, the part of the line intercepted between them is also necessarily the line of shortest descent with regard to them." [19] This does not exhaust the interesting characteristics of this curve. If from any position on the curve a particle is released, and constrained to travel by frictionless rolling along the curve under the force of gravity (and the normal force exerted by contact with the curve), the particle will reach the bottom of the curve in the *same* amount of time regardless of the initial point selected (excepting the bottom point itself, of course). Thus

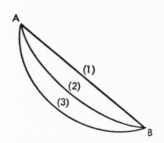

[17] At first glance it might seem that a straight line, (1), yields the required curve. But it is clear that the particle would gain a greater velocity if it started with somewhat of a drop, as in (2), and thus more than compensate for the longer path by its greater speed. On the other hand if the initial drop were too steep, as in (3), the advantage of gained speed would yield to the disadvantage of added distance.

[18] *Math.*, III, p. 303. Cf. n. 10 of the section on the principle of perfection. Moritz Cantor is imprecise in stating (*G. d. Math.*, III, p. 225), that the name "Brachystochrone" for this curve first occurs in John Bernouilli's solution of the problem in the *Acta Eruditorum* of May 1697. Bernouilli had used the term earlier in a letter communicating his own solution to Leibniz which is dated July 1696 (*Math.*, III, pp. 295 ff.) from which we learn that the curve was almost destined to get another name. Here he writes: "I had given the line the name of 'Brachystochrone' for the reason you see here, but if the name 'Tachystoptote' is more pleasing, I permit that it be used anywhere in the place of the former."

[19] *Phil.*, VII, p. 272.

the curve is also a tauto- or iso-chrone, a property which Huygens had already discovered by 1665.[20]

The noteworthy point is that in all problems of this sort belonging to the branch of mathematics now called the *calculus of variations,* the object is *to find one among an infinite number of alternative paths that achieves an extremization (minimization or maximization) of some specified characteristic* (time, distance, and so on). What is at issue in such physical problems is an infinite comparison process leading to selection of an optimal alternative.

In his doctrine of contingence, perhaps more heavily than in any other part of his philosophy, Leibniz the philosopher is indebted to Leibniz the mathematician. The logic underlying this doctrine stems entirely and directly from Leibniz' mathematical investigations:

> There is something which had perplexed me for a long time—how it is possible for the predicate of a proposition to be contained in *(inesse)* the subject without making the proposition necessary. But the knowledge of Geometrical matters, and especially of infinitesimal analysis, lit the lamp for me, so that I came to see that notions too can be resolvable *in infinitum*.[21]

> At length some new and unexpected light appeared from a direction in which my hopes were smallest—from mathematical considerations regarding the nature of the infinite. In truth there are two labyrinths in the human mind, one concerning the composition of the continuum, the other concerning the nature of freedom. And both of these spring from exactly the same source—the infinite.[22]

Contingentiae Radix

We must now deal with a point which has troubled many commentators on Leibniz, and, regarded as perhaps the weakest spot in his defenses, has been one of the most prominent objects of attack by Leibniz' critics. The matter consists of a supposed conflict between God's freedom and perfection and the Principle of Suf-

---

[20] See Moritz Cantor, *Vorlesungen über Geschichte der Mathematik,* III (Leipzig: B. G. Teuber, 1880–1898), pp. 133-34.

[21] Couturat, *Opuscules,* p. 18.

[22] Couturat, *Logique,* p. 210, notes.

ficient Reason. It can be formulated in a dilemma. According to the Principle of Perfection God acts in the most perfect way possible with regard to the creation of the world, and He does so either necessarily or freely. If He does so necessarily His freedom is destroyed, and all that follows as a result of His perfection—i.e., everything that happens in the world—is necessary. If He does so freely, in accord with Leibniz' principle, a sufficient reason must be adduced for this free act, and this in turn must be either free or necessitated. Thus an infinite regress is initiated.

Russell hangs Leibniz on the first horn of the dilemma.[23] He views Leibniz' system as *au fond* necessitarian, and regards the painfully drawn distinction between the necessary and contingent truths as null and void.[24] He charges Leibniz' system with involving that universal necessitation which its author was so ready to decry in Spinoza.

Although this problem is central to the philosophy of Leibniz, he never discusses it as fully and explicitly as one could desire. Still he did deal with, and to his own satisfaction solved, the problem of the reconciliation of God's freedom with the principle of sufficient reason.[25] This reconciliation, so necessary to Leibniz' system,[26] is to be regarded as one of its *tours de force*.

It is important to eliminate an ambiguity in Leibniz' word *perfection,* an equivocation of which Leibniz himself was aware. Perfection in one sense is quantity of essence, potentiality for existence. Let us call this *metaphysical perfection*. God, who exists necessarily as we have seen, *is in this sense* wholly and necessarily perfect. But the word *perfection* when used in connection with God has another

---

23 Bertrand Russell, *Critical Exposition*, p. 39, n. 1; cf. his paper in *Mind*, vol. 12 (1903), pp. 177-201, especially p. 185, n. 2.

24 Falsely, since this distinction is drawn on logical grounds alone.

25 See the opuscule *De Contingentia* (Grua, *Textes*, I, pp. 302-8).

26 This is so since God's freedom is one of the central tenets of Leibniz' philosophy. "God is always infallibly led to the best although He is not led necessarily (other than by a moral necessity) . . . , it was not necessary or essential that God should create [a world], nor that God should create this world in particular, although His wisdom and goodness led Him to it" [*Phil.*, III, p. 402; letter to Coste (1707)]. Thus in Objection 8 of the *Abrégé en forme* of the *Théodicée* Leibniz criticizes the argument:

"Whoever cannot fail to choose the best, is not free.
God cannot fail to choose the best.

Hence, God is not free."

Leibniz answers: "I deny the major premise of this argument" (*Phil.*, VI, pp. 385-86).

sense, more akin to *goodness,* and this is the sense used in the expression *Principle of Perfection.* God's perfectly good conduct in the creation of the world is logically distinct from His metaphysical perfection, and we will term it His *moral perfection.* Leibniz holds that God is of necessity metaphysically perfect, but He is morally perfect by free choice. The desire to preserve God's freedom is the motivation for Leibniz' definition of God, not as the *perfect,* but as the *necessary* being, i.e., as perfect metaphysically, but not, by definition, morally.

Not only does Leibniz' world have contingent features, unlike that of Spinoza, but even Leibniz' God is the bearer of contingent attributes—all those which relate, not to His existence or knowledge or power, but to His *will,* i.e., His choices regarding the world of His creation. In all respects relating to God's agency (not His capacities for agency but His actual exercise thereof) God is free and all the relevant truths, including that of the principle "God is good," are contingent.

We can now face the problem of the freedom of God's moral perfection, and resolve our difficulty as follows. God's moral perfection follows from His metaphysical perfection, but the deduction would require an infinity of steps. God's moral perfection has a sufficient reason, and this in turn a sufficient reason, and so on *ad infinitum*—an infinite regress which converges on God's metaphysical perfection. Such an infinite regress is not vicious, but is essential if universal necessitation is to be avoided.

Thus Leibniz would deal with the dilemma with which we initially presented him by accepting, and indeed insisting on the truth of, the second horn. Infinite processes can be accomplished by God in a way comprehensible to us only analogically, by means of infinite series and the calculus.

The Principle of Perfection, being a contingent truth,[27] *must* itself involve an infinite regress of sufficient reasons.[28] Analysis of the contingent must lead to the necessary, i.e., to God *qua* meta-

---

27 The Principle of Perfection is itself the cardinal and primary contingent truth, for all that exists contingently does so ". . . by the free decrees of the divine will, of which the primary one is the decision to do everything in the best possible way, as seems wisest" (*Phil.,* VII, pp. 309-10, notes).

28 "A true contingent proposition cannot be reduced to an identity but is nonetheless tested by showing with continued greater and greater resolution that it indeed approaches identity perpetually, but never reaches it" (Couturat, *Opuscules,* p. 388).

physically perfect.[29] Hence God's moral perfection must be grounded in His metaphysical perfection, but the derivation of the former from the latter requires an infinity of steps. It is by means of *the infinite* that Leibniz reconciles God's freedom and perfection with the Principle of Sufficient Reason,[30] and this problem of reconciliation, instead of being the weak spot of Leibniz' philosophy, provides the key to its inner sanctum—the infinitistic character of the contingent: *Contingentiae radix est in infinitum* ("The ground of contingency is in the infinite").

---

29 "But this progression to infinity (of the analysis of truths of fact) has the locus of its cause . . . outside the series (of truths of contingence in God . . ." (*Phil.*, VII, p. 200). "It is evident from these considerations that the ultimate extraworldly reason of things, or God, cannot be escaped by means of a postulated eternity of the world," or "These considerations show clearly that we cannot escape an ultimate extramundane reason for things, or God, even by assuming the eternity of the world" (*Phil.*, VII, p. 303). "If the necessary Being is possible, he exists. For the necessary Being and the Being-by-his-essence are one and the same thing. . . . If the Being-through-self is impossible, all beings through others are so too, since they only are, in the end, through the Being-through-self: and thus nothing could exist" (*Phil.*, IV, p. 406). "If there were no necessary being, there would be no contingent being" (*Phil.*, VII, p. 310).

30 "The root cause of contingency is in the infinite: A contingent truth is one which is indemonstrable" (Couturat, *Opuscules,* p. 212, n. 2).

four

FOUR SUBSIDIARY
PRINCIPLES

Preliminaries

This chapter will deal with four important subsidiary principles which play a prominent part in Leibniz' philosophy. It is not meant to suggest that these subsidiary principles are intrinsically less important or interesting than other, nonsubsidiary principles. They merit this appellation only in the logicians' use of the term, in that they are inferentially *derivative* from the principles characterized as fundamental.

The Identity of Indiscernibles

The Principle of the Identity of Indiscernibles was formulated by Leibniz in many different ways in different contexts: "No two substances are completely similar, or differ solely in number." [1]

---

[1] *Phil.*, IV, p. 433.

"There are not in nature two indiscernible real absolute beings." [2] In some of these formulations it might appear as though the principle applied only to the substances of *this,* i.e., the real, world, and failed to hold for other possible worlds. This impression would be mistaken, because this logically grounded, metaphysically necessary principle holds good in every possible world. In its logical formulation, the principle reads, apart from a confusion of use and mention, exactly like a rule of substitution for identicals in modern systems of logic: *Eadem sunt quorum unum in alterius locum substitui potest, salva veritate* ["Things are the same (or *identical*) one of which can be substituted in place of the other with preservation of truth"].[3] There can be no doubt that Leibniz did have in mind such a logical principle, analytically explicative of the very concept of identity.

Leibniz did not hesitate to put a metaphysical construction upon this logical principle: If, of two possible things, #1 could be put in place of thing #2 in such a way that the world is left wholly intact—the truth of every proposition about it being unaffected—then things #1 and #2 are not two things but must be one and the same thing identified by different labels. The foundation for this metaphysical thesis is purely logical. A substance (i.e., possible substance) is characterized by its complete description, its individual notion. Where there is only one such notion there is only one possible substance, since that individual concept is *its* concept. A substance, prior to its actualization, subsists as a conceptual possibility in the mind of God. To arrive at another substance we would have to contemplate a change in the concept, altering the description at issue. The logical rationale of the situation that might be summarized by observing that the purely logical or conceptual dictum "one concept—one substance" finishes the grounding of Leibniz' Principle of the Identity of Indiscernibles. Since the substances realized are chosen from among those whose defining concepts are entertained by God *sub ratione possibilitatis,* and since a substance so considered can only be considered in terms of its predicates (since there is nothing else to individuate an individual concept), it is plain that distinct substances must in at least some

---

2 *Phil.,* VII, p. 393.

3 *Ibid.,* p. 219. The principle so formulated might be construed either as the thesis $x = y \equiv (\emptyset) [\emptyset x \equiv \emptyset y]$ or as the rule: If $x = y$ then from $\emptyset x$ we may infer $\emptyset y$, for any $\emptyset$; and conversely.

respect differ in their properties, and thus have distinct predicates. Leibniz explicitly and repeatedly holds the Principle of the Identity of Indiscernibles to be derivative from the Principle of Sufficient Reason: "I own that if two things perfectly indiscernible from each other did exist, they would be two [distinct things]; but that supposition is false, and contrary to the grand principle of reason." [4] The reasoning here is readily understood: If there were two distinct indiscernibles a and b, then there would have to be present in the complete individual notion of substance a a truth regarding it—namely, that there are several other substances answering exactly to its own description—which could not reasonably be held to be something programmed into the concept of a, since b is conceptually indistinguishable from a. The principle should thus be regarded as grounded in the Principle of Identity, in view of the fact that it is conceptually explicative of the notion of identity.

It should be remarked, however, that, while the Principle of the Identity of Indiscernibles is necessarily applicable to all substances, it need not, and should not, be taken as necessarily applicable to phenomena.[5] That two like objects might be indistinguishable to humans operating with limited means for observational discrimination could be granted by Leibniz as unproblematic for his system. He does not have to hold that all things are distinguished, but only that they are *distinguishable*—discriminable, in the final analysis, by God, who alone knows the complete individual notions of the substances at issue.

An Objection to the Preceding Principle

Bertrand Russell has argued as follows:

> If a substance is *only* defined by its predicates—and this is essential to the Identity of Indiscernibles—then it would seem to be identical with the sum of those predicates. In that case, to say that such and such a substance exists is merely a compendious way of saying that all its predicates exist. . . . But this . . . is not what Leibniz intends to say. The substance is a single simple indivisible thing . . . ;

---

4 *Phil.*, VII, pp. 371-72, 394-95.
5 See Chap. 7.

it is not the same as the series of its states [predicates], but is the subject of them. But in this case, a substance is not properly speaking *defined* by its predicates.[6]

This counterargument of Russell's breaks down because he refuses to take proper notice of the distinction between *the definition of a thing* (i.e., the formula that provides its individual defining concept), and *the (corresponding) thing defined*. The thing is of course different from the individual *concept* that defines it (else how could the question of its *creation* arise?), although it answers to it fully, in every respect, since the defining concept provides a *complete* description of the thing defined. The individual concept of a substance is not like a blueprint or an architect's drawing in specifying only an incomplete set of descriptive details about the thing at issue, so that a plurality of items could be made corresponding to the plan. Russell fails to take seriously Leibniz' insistence that the individual concept of a thing be complete and specify every detail about this thing. This is the reason why two or more distinct substances cannot correspond to one individual concept.

The Principle of Plenitude

What I shall call the Principle of Plenitude—it might also be called the Principle of Existence-Maximization—is a reasonably immediate consequence of Leibniz' Principle of Perfection. Let us reconsider the workings of that principle somewhat more closely. In accord with it, the world as a whole is as perfect as possible. There are not, as with Descartes, partial imperfections compensated for by the perfection of the whole. Each part of the world aids in the maximization of perfection by contributing the maximum of perfection possible for it.[7] The immediate consequence of the Principle of Perfection is that God actualized that possible world in which perfection is at a maximum. God is perfect, consequently the only outlet for that perfection—the world—is perfect. Within the limits of possibility the actual world contains the most perfection. It suffices only to add the premise that existence is a mode of

---

6 Bertrand Russell, *Critical Exposition of the Philosophy of Leibniz* (London: George Allen & Unwin Ltd., 1937), p. 59.
7 See pp. 26-27.

perfection to obtain the consequence that the actual world is such that the "quantity of existence" is maximized within the "best of possible worlds."

There is thus in Leibniz' metaphysic a Principle of Plenitude, that is, of "existence-maximization," linked to, and indeed immediately derivative from, the Principle of Perfection.

The Law of Continuity
("Lex Continuitatis")

The notion of continuity has application wherever a concept of *nearness* is provided, and the question *Do the objects in the neighborhood of a given object possess such and such a property?* can be raised meaningfully. Though applicable in many contexts,[8] this nearness has historically been of primarily two sorts, spatial and temporal. Let us consider the part played by the notion of continuity in the philosophy of Leibniz.[9]

In 1687 Leibniz formulated a principle based on mathematical considerations which he termed the law of continuity,[10] to the effect that, when in the solution of problems the differences in data diminish, so do the differences in the results obtained from these data; when the former go to zero the latter follow suit. This principle, Leibniz maintains, "depends on a yet more general principle, namely: as the data ordered, so the unknowns are ordered also." [11]

---

[8] E.g., "nearness" taken as similarity in shade, or in tone, or in any other qualitative respect.

[9] In mathematical analysis the continuity properties of functions play an important role, and there is little doubt that it was his mathematical studies which suggested to Leibniz the philosophic potentialities of the continuity concept.

[10] "Lex continuitatis" or "principe de continuité." See *Phil.*, III, pp. 51-55 (1687); *Math.*, VII, pp. 260 ff., esp. 266-71 (probably 1687); and also Couturat, *Logique*, p. 398, n. It is conceivable that Leibniz had continuity considerations in mind when he rejected the perfectly elastic impact *of particles,* and hence atomism, since a discontinuity is involved here. The time of this rejection, the stay in Paris, adds plausibility to this. However, it is probable that Leibniz had not formulated a *principle* of continuity considerably prior to its first formulation in print in 1687. The polemics against the Cartesians of 1686 would have called for its invocation had it been available then.

[11] *Phil.*, III, p. 52. Cf. the opuscule translated by P. P. Wiener in *Leibniz: Selections* (New York: Charles Scribner's Sons, 1951), pp. 65-70.

The application for the sake of which the first formulation in the principle took place was the revelation of an error in the laws of motion as given by Descartes.[12]

Even in its first presentation [13] this law of continuity was presented by Leibniz as a consequence of the Principle of Perfection. The derivation is based on the line of thought that, by embodiment of continuity among its constituents, a possible world exhibits one of the modes of perfection. As usual when he is in possession of a useful mathematical or physical principle, Leibniz applies it in philosophy, where it is given the formulation: "Jumps are forbidden not only in motions, but also in every order of things and of truths." [14] Let us next examine these instances of continuity and applications of the continuity principle of Leibniz' philosophy.

A. Continuity in the realm of monads

1. From the very first the monad is presented as a perduring substance.[15] In mathematical jargon a one-parameter family of states is involved,[16] and this change of state of a substance (appetition) is continuous.

2. At any instant every monad represents the entire universe from its own point of view with varying degrees of clarity.[17] This makes possible a twofold continuous distribution of the monads. a) In *point of view*—it is always possible to find a monad differing from a given monad in point of view by less than any preassigned difference. This is basic to the Leibnizian theory of space, and to his denial of a vacuum. b) In *perfection* [18]—determined in terms of

---

[12] "Which has served me for a long time as a principle of invention in physics, and also as a very convenient test to see if certain given rules work well." *Phil.*, III, p. 52.

[13] *Ibid.*

[14] *Ibid.*, p. 635.

[15] See DM and the correspondence with Arnauld.

[16] "The complete or perfect notion (concept) of a singular (individual) substance involves all its predicates, past, present, and future."

[17] "All singular [L has *individual*] created substances are diverse expressions of the same universe, but the expressions vary in perfection."

[18] I.e., in clarity of perception or adequacy of representation. See *Phil.*, VII, p. 535.

clarity of perception the varying degrees of which thus effect a continuous ordering of the system of monads.[19]

3. The monads are also continuously ordered with regard to *structure*. As Russell puts it, "If two substances differ by a finite difference there must be . . . a continuous series of intermediate substances, each of which differs infinitesimally from the next.[20] In this way Leibniz denies what he terms a "vacuum formarum." [21]

Thus continuity enters in Leibniz' metaphysical world in monadic structure, viewpoint, appetition, and perfection.

B. *Continuity in the physical world*

1. The monadic aggregates of the physical world are of two kinds, those well founded phenomena that are no more than mere phenomena, and "true unities." The aggregates with unity, the living beings,[22] are continuously ordered with respect to the perfection of their dominant monad. All creatures are linked in a "liaison universelle." [23] This leads also to the continuity of the species of living beings.[24]

2. It proceeds from considerations concerning monads that physical space is a plenum.[25] This is mentioned here in passing, for we shall have more to say later about the nature of physical space as conceived by Leibniz.

3. All the processes of the physical world (motion, impact, and so on) take place continuously, according to Leibniz.[26] To put the

---

[19] Consequently we find Leibniz saying that the monads are ordered "comme autant d'Ordonnées s'une même Courbe, dont l'union ne souffre pas, qu'on place d'autres entre deux, à cause que cela marqueroit du désordre et de l'imperfection" [Guhrauer, *Leibniz,* Vol. I (Breslau: F. Hirt, 1846), Anmerkungen, p. 32].

[20] Russell, *Critical Exposition,* pp. 64-65.

[21] *Phil.,* II, p. 168; *Phil.,* VI, p. 548; *Nouv. Ess.,* III, Chap. 4, §13.

[22] For present purposes we can adopt the view held by Leibniz in some passages that all animals, even the lowest, may be regarded as true unities.

[23] *Phil.,* IV, p. 546; *Nouv. Ess.,* IV, Chap. 21, §12.

[24] Gubrauer, *op. cit.,* pp. 32-33.

[25] See point 2 of section A. Cf. *Monadology,* §§66-69.

[26] See, for example, the discussion of motion in Leibniz' *Dynamica* (*Math.,* VI, pp. 320-26).

matter as briefly as possible, the principle of continuity as applied to the physical world is nothing but the classical principle *natura non facit saltus*.

C. Other occurrences of continuity in the philosophy of Leibniz

Here, primary in the theory of knowledge and in psychology, is the famous doctrine of the "little perception." As a corollary to this doctrine the continuity of life in sleep, unconsciousness, and even in death is obtained. The little perceptions are also invoked to explain the continuity of change in conscious thought. Using them as a starting point, Leibniz establishes an elaborate psychology involving "petites dégagements," and an "inquietude" composed of "petites solicitations." [27] By means of these the continuity of the passions is demonstrated; for example, just as rest is an infinitesimal motion so joy is an infinitesimal sorrow.[28] It is remarkable how thoroughly the principle of continuity is diffused throughout the philosophy of Leibniz.[29]

Regarding the Law of Continuity, Russell writes: "This law usually holds a prominent place in expositions of Leibniz, but I cannot discover that, except as applied to Mathematics, it has any great importance." [30] Such slight valuation of the principle of continuity is misguided, for the principle not only holds a prominent place in expositions of Leibniz, it holds one in the metaphysical system of Leibniz as well. Indeed, it provides, as we shall see, one of the fundamental bases for Leibniz' entire theory of space and time, and moreover is, as we have said, the foundation of his psychological theory.

---

27 *Nouv. Ess.*, II, Chap. 20, §§2, 6.
28 See G. Wanke, *Das Stetigkeitsgesetz bein Leibniz* (Kiel: Die Universität, 1892), especially p. 30.
29 "Francis of Borgia, General of the Jesuits, who has at last been canonized, being wont to drink largely when he was a man in high life, reduced himself little by little upon a small scale, when he thought of retiring (from the world), by causing a drop of wax to fall daily into the bottle which he was wont to empty" (*Nouv. Ess.;* tr. Langley, p. 191).
30 Russell, *Critical Exposition*, p. 63.

The Pre-Established Harmony

Leibniz distinguishes between the actual world and various other possible worlds. Equally important is a further distinction which splits the actual world into two domains: the realm of monads, the real world, which forms the object of study of metaphysics; and the realm of the things of our everyday experience, the phenomenal world, which forms the object of study of the sciences in general, but pre-eminently of physics. These two realms, physical and metaphysical, are not disparate or disjoint, but are different aspects of the same world. The system of phenomena results from the system of monads, and is well founded in it.

The notion of well founding, and the several theories by which it is implemented, occupies a central position in Leibniz' thought. Here, at the joining of physics and metaphysics, we shall have occasion later for detailed investigations. At the moment let it suffice to remark that the main instrument for well founding, providing the means for explaining phenomena in terms of monads, is the pre-established harmony. It explains how similarities and uniformities arise among monads, and thus accounts for the behavior of monadic aggregates, and for their relation to individual monads.

A word must be said concerning the pre-established harmony in its own right. It is a *harmony* that obtains among the monads, not a mutual causal influence, because every individual substance is self-complete, and its development in time is fixed. No causal relations can arise among monads; at best they can *accord* with one another in their states. This protocausal reciprocal accord extends throughout the universe and links all of its monads in one vast framework of mutual interrelation. We humans may lose sight of this

> because our senses lead us to judge only superficially, but in reality, because of the interconnection of things, the entire universe, with all of its parts, would be wholly different, and would have been another world altogether from its very commencement, if the least thing in it happened otherwise than it has.[31]

---

[31] *Phil.*, II, p. 62.

This accord is *pre*-established in a dual sense: first because it is determined upon anterior to the creation of the world, second because the accord at any instant of time is but the consequence of the accord at any previous instant. These interconnections are of an intimate linkage that continues operative in infinite detail throughout the course of historical development of the universe:

> All singular things [i.e., substances] are successive . . . nor is there anything permanent in them, on my view, except that law itself which involves this continued succession, agreeing in singulars with [all] that which is in the whole universe.[32]

The fact that the actual world is such that a thoroughgoing network of agreement and accord obtains among its constituents is not a necessary result. It represents a mode of perfection of this world, not an inevitable feature of every possible world. It is a contingent truth—one that obtains by virtue of the Principle of Perfection—that a Pre-Established Harmony reigns among the constituent substances of the actual world.

It is important for an understanding of Leibniz to distinguish between *compossibility* and *harmony*. The mutual compossibility of the substances of this actual, and/or any other possible, world is a metaphysically necessary feature: the purely logical mutual accord in the minimal sense of mutual compatibility is logically inevitable. But the fact that its substances harmonize with one another in a manner far beyond mere logical compatibility to make for a genuine intricately articulate *cosmos* (a world governed by simple, general, and universal principles of physical and psychological order) is among the features that make this "the best possible world."

Summary

With the exception of the Principle of the Identity of Indiscernibles, which derives from the Principle of Sufficient Reason, the subsidiary principles we have considered in this chapter are all derivative consequences of the Principle of Perfection. The fundamental ideas of Leibniz' philosophy can thus be set forth, as we

---

[32] *Phil.*, II, p. 263.

have endeavored to do in this and the preceding chapters, in terms of an architectonic grouping of principles, as follows:

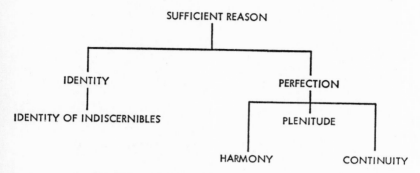

Leibniz can claim for his philosophical system the sort of perfection at issue in his ontology: richness of detail articulated within a unifying framework of principles of order.

five

THE REALM OF MONADS
AND ITS CREATION

How the Realm of Monads Differs
from Other Possible Worlds

As Leibniz looked at it, the actual world, the realm of created monads, is but one of infinite possible worlds. It is, however, a very special one, the one unique alternative selected for realization or actualization (actual creation) on the basis of its possession of a certain special feature which distinguishes it from the other, alternative possible worlds. This feature, of course, is its greater perfection. (The degree of perfection of a possible world is determined, for Leibniz, by two factors: its *variety,* as manifested in the richness of its phenomena, and its *orderliness,* as manifested in the simplicity of its laws.) In view of its perfection, and specifically of its orderliness, the actual world exhibits in great measure two features which Leibniz regards as having central importance: *continuity* and *harmony.* (We have already considered these Leibnizian themes at some length in the preceding chapter.) Its possession of these modes of order in a relatively greater degree than all other possible worlds that are even close to the content richness of ours serves to set the actual world apart from its possible competitors.

The continuity and harmony inherent in the design of the actual world assure that it exhibits orderliness at both a private and a public level of consideration. At the *private* level, each single monad, considered individually, exhibits continuity and harmony entering into the assemblage of mutually contemporaneous factors which constitute one specific state of a monad, and into the state-to-state transition (appetition) characteristic of monadic change; there is no passage from state to state without intervening passage through the intermediate states. At the *public* level, continuity and harmony again enter into the entire system of monads in the constitution of mutually contemporaneous states which constitute an inter-monadic "time-slice" running across the system of monads, and in the macro-changes in monadic complexes. This summary characterization is but a rough sketch that needs development and refinement.

Monadic Perceptions and Their Transition (i.e., Appetition)

The philosophy of Leibniz, like that of Descartes or Spinoza, centers about a characteristic conception of substance. The prime features of Leibniz' conception of substance are 1) that a given individual substance is a simple, perduring existent, not in the sense of logical simplicity, but in the absence of spatial parts; and 2) that a given individual substance is capable of functioning as the subject of propositions, the predicates of true propositions concerning the substance standing for attributes of the substance. Speaking generally, one can describe Leibniz' individual substance as a spatio-temporal continuant, an existent without spatial parts, but not without attributes, and with a perduring individuality and an inner dynamic of change.

Let us call the state of affairs corresponding to a consistent total description of the attributes of a substance the *state* of the substance at a given moment. We can be certain that this description characterizes an instantaneous (contemporaneous) state of the substance for, as we shall see, the family of attributes of a substance is in constant flux, and its attribute-family over a noninstantaneous period in the history of a substance would be logically inconsistent. That a monad, substance within the actual world, has many different states is an aspect of variety; that these states are continuously orderable into smooth transitional sequences is an aspect of orderliness.

The internal programming of the monads built into their complete individual notion (as into that of every other possible substance) is the basis for the state-to-state transition that makes them unstable and ever-changing. This feature of monads—that a created monad is changing, with each of its new states but a prelude to others—leads Leibniz to the metaphor that "the present is pregnant with the future." Each individual substance is subject to a perpetual change of state; such changes are without jumps, the transition of the substance from one state to another being always continuous. Continuous change from one system of perceptions to another is the only "activity" of which an individual substance is capable.[1] Leibniz chooses to call it *appetition*, defining it as "the tendency from one perception to another,"[2] but the dangerous connotations of this term in the direction of active, and above all conscious, seeking or striving must be avoided. The duality, reminiscent of the curve-equations in Cartesian coordinates, of the "law of development," and the development itself, are deeply ingrained into Leibniz' concept of appetition. His retention of both intensional and extensional interpretations of logic is significant for his theory of individual substance as answering to both a *determinative conception* or *law* (the complete individual notion) and the *continuing series*

---

[1] We have not spoken of "force" as associated with individual substances, nor made much of Leibniz' much-touted "dynamism." This is because "force" in the philosophy of Leibniz is a derived notion, resulting from perceptions and their changes. Leibnizian *dynamism*, or the doctrine of unextended centers of force, ill describes Leibniz' theory of substance, for his individual substances are a good deal more than this label suggests.

[2] *Phil.*, III, p. 575.

of particular events or perceptions which are the instantiations of this concept.

It should be remarked that having many states and distinct states at distinct "times" is a logically necessary feature of every possible substance (derived partly from the very concept of a possible substance itself, and partly from the Principle of the Identity of Indiscernibles). However, the contingent fact that monadic change is smooth and orderly—i.e., continuous—and, more generally, that the world is a harmonious *cosmos,* not a *chaos,* is inherent in the Principle of Perfection.

Perception, Representation, "Causality"

One of the consequences of the pre-established harmony is that, to any instantaneous state of a given individual substance there corresponds, in a certain fashion, exactly one instantaneous state of every other individual substance. Such an instantaneous "contemporaneity-slice" cutting through the history of all substances defines a moment of *time.* (The time-order of the universe is a feature of this best possible world, not a logically necessary feature of any possible world as such.) Thus at any moment of time each substance "perceives" or "represents" or "expresses" all the others, in the sense that a certain similarity relationship obtains between their states. The universal correspondence established by the mutual perceptions is the result, not of any mutual causal interaction, but of a divinely ordained accord, the pre-established harmony.[3] Each substance is not "represented" or "perceived" or "expressed" by every other substance in an equally sharp and detailed way. There are varying degrees of clarity, and inversely of confusion, in "perception," and so, as Leibniz graphically put it, "Every mind is omniscient but confused."[4] Each substance perceives more clearly those substances closer to, or more important for, it.[5] Thus each

---

3 Being a mechanist, Leibniz could not admit instantaneous causal influence at a distance.

4 L. Couturat, *Opuscules,* p. 10.

5 For the principles governing the clarity of perception see *Phil.,* II, p. 90, and *Monadology,* §60.

substance perceives the whole universe from its own special point of view, and this is the basis for the spatial relationships among substances. (Note that in this way both spatiality and temporality are essential to *any* possible universe which involves a plurality of mtually according substances with changing states, and are not confined to this existing universe.)

Leibniz flatly states that there is nothing whatever to substances over and above concurrent perceptions and their chronological appetitions from one perception to another.[6] Does this mean that a monad has no autonomous properties characteristic of it as such, without being reflective of another? Is the realm of monads a shadow world of perceptions of perceptions of perceptions, *ad indefinitum,* a perpetual being-for-others without any being-of-itself? Of course not! A Leibnizian "perception" is not merely other-reflective but strictly intrinsic, a matter of *accord* or *similarity* between orthodoxly qualitative properties. The fact that all of a monad's properties agree with those of others does make all of them into perceptions, but does not prevent them from being—in Leibniz' view *requires* them to be—genuinely internal properties, not simply shadowy reflections of the (equally shadowy) properties of others.

Since *representation* is, for Leibniz, the inverse of *perception* (*A* is represented in *B* insofar as *B* perceives *A*), substantial light can be shed upon monadic perception from the angle of Leibniz' treatment of representation. Writing to Arnauld, Leibniz explains representation in the following terms:

> One thing *expresses* another, in my use of the term, when there is a constant and regulated relation between what can be said [i.e., *predicated*] of the one and of the other. It is thus that a projection in perspective expresses a geometric figure.[7]

Things thus represent one another, to the extent that a structural

---

6 ". . . nothing but this—namely perceptions and their changes—can be found in a simple substance" (*Monadology,* §17). ". . . any one Monad in itself and at a particular moment can be distinguished from any other only by internal qualities and activities, which cannot be other than its *perceptions* (that is to say, the representation of the compound, or of that which is outside, in the simple) and its *appetitions* (that is to say, its tendencies to pass from one perception to another), which are the principles of change" (PNG, §2).

7 *Phil.,* II, p. 112.

agreement obtains between them. This is not a strictly reciprocal matter, like ordinary similarity, because one represents the other more fully than the reverse when the structure they commonly exhibit is more clearly and distinctly defined in one than in the other.

Since all monads are fundamentally alike, in that every monad perceives everything else in the universe, a question can be raised as to how they can possibly differ from one another. Leibniz seems to think in terms of the analogy of painting, of two different depictions of exactly the same scene. Monads, he says, differ from one another not in what they perceive, but 1) in *point of view*, i.e., with differing features of the things they perceive; and 2) in *clearness of perception*, i.e., with differing faithfulness of representation of the various aspects of things. Leibniz thus replies to the question of the present paragraph as follows:

> It is not in the objects represented that the monads are limited, but in the modification of their knowledge of the object. In a confused way they all reach out to infinity or to the whole, but are limited and differentiated in the degrees of their distinct perceptions.[8]

Although monadic perception is basically determined in terms of similarity, the relationship at issue is not actually a symmetric one, for certainly monad A can perceive monad B more clearly than B perceives A. The best way to think of the matter is in pictographic terms: A and B perceive the same thing, but A perceives it more sharply than B does.

The Creation

Each possible substance possesses a greater or lesser degree of perfection proportionally with its being capable of greater or lesser clarity in perceiving its fellows in the possible world of which it is a member. The merit or worthiness of the substance for actualization, its quantity of essence or potentiality for existence, is directly proportional to its perfection. God, desirous to act in the most perfect possible way, actualizes that possible world constituted by that

---

8 *Monadology*, §60.

system of possible substances for which the sum total of perfection is at a maximum. On the basis of God's own perfection, each possible substance has a "claim" to existence in accordance with its own perfection and that of its possible world, giving it a "drive towards existence."

It becomes possible to appreciate the general direction of Leibniz' exculpation of God from blame for evil and imperfection as they seem to exist in the world. Each substance has "always" subsisted, or, strictly speaking, has had a conceptual mode of being that lies outside of time altogether—*sub ratione possibilitatis*. Its total nature was determined, for its adequate and complete notion (i.e., all of its predicates save *existence*) was fixed.[9] For this nature God is in no way responsible; it is an object of his understanding, and no creature of his will. For actualization God chose the best (i.e., most perfect) system of compossible substances, thus he is the reason for all existence, hence for all existent perfection and imperfection. Imperfection is not avoidable since, by the identity of indiscernibles, no substance different from God can be wholly perfect. God, however, chose to minimize imperfection, or rather, positively, to maximize perfection. He is positively the cause of existent perfection, but only negatively of imperfection, since he retained only what could not but remain. This is how Leibniz accounts for imperfection in the best of all possible worlds.

---

[9] "The complete or perfect notion of a singular substance involves all its predicates, past, present, and future" (Couturat, *Opuscules*, p. 520; cf. *ibid.*, p. 403). That existence is not among these predicates follows from the fact that the complete notion of possible substances was completely determined and accessible to the mind of God anterior to any decisions of creation (cf. *Phil.*, II, p. 50). It is therefore clear that existence, if a predicate at all for Leibniz, is a very exceptional one, which cannot in the nature of things enter into the complete individual notion (essence) of any substance save God alone. Thus Leibniz remarks on the margin of a ms. which cannot possibly antedate 1686, "If existence were anything other than what essence demands, then it would follow that it has an essence of some sort, and would add something new to things, of which one might in turn ask whether this essence exists, and why this [exists] rather than something else" (*Phil.*, VII, p. 195). And I by no means agree with Russell who regards *Phil.*, V, p. 339 as establishing conclusively that Leibniz held existence to be a predicate (Russell, *Critical Exposition* [London: George Allen & Unwin Ltd., 1937], pp. 27, 174, 185). Indeed in this passage Leibniz seems to be concerned with reducing existence from the status of a real characteristic to that of an *ens rationis*, like relations.

It remains to say a word as to the nature of Leibniz' concept of creation. Commenting on his statement, that "One can define *an existent* as that which is compatible with more than anything else which is incompatible with it," [10] Russell holds that:

> Strange consequences follow if Leibniz intended this to be, in a strict sense, a definition of "existence." For, if it was so intended there was no act of Creation. . . . This world, it would follow, exists by definition without the need of any Divine Decree.[11]

Since Leibniz held that existence cannot be accounted for without a reliance upon divine decrees, the above is not, strictly speaking, to be taken as a definition, but its status in the logical development of Leibniz' system is that of a *theorem*, i.e., a derivative principle. It is, in fact, an immediate corollary of the Principle of Perfection—a principle obtaining in virtue of a divine decree. Thus Russell is right that, strictly speaking, there is no *definition* at issue here.

Russell is also right in holding that it is difficult to find a place in Leibniz' cosmology for an historical "act" of creation; Leibniz' *creation* can in no sense be an historical event. There was no moment of time when the universe was not, for time itself is logically posterior to the existence of the universe. Further, an act of creation would seem to require a first instant in the history of the thing created, and Leibniz, though he inclines toward the view that there is a first moment of time, is by no means dogmatic on this point.[12] Had Leibniz conceived of the creation in a quasi-historical fashion, he would doubtless have been firmer on this point. We thus arrive at the conclusion that Leibniz regarded God as a necessary condition for the existence of a world, but that it would be an error to attribute to him any view of an historical act of creation. To speak of anything prior to the existent universe is to use the term in a purely logical, not temporal sense, and when doing so one deals with the necessary being, the necessary truths, and the possible worlds, entering the sphere of pure logic, where it is hardly possible to find a place for activity of any sort.

---

10 Couturat, *Opuscules,* p. 360.
11 Russell, *Critical Exposition,* p. vi.
12 In a later chapter we will deal with Leibniz' theories of time, and evidence for these statements will be presented.

The Existence of God

It is universally agreed that Leibniz held God's existence to be necessary, but the characteristically Leibnizian proof of the existence of God is often overlooked. It is, for example, put into the shade in Russell's discussion, following that of Erdmann, of four such proofs offered by Leibniz—the Anselmio-Cartesian Ontological Argument, the Cosmological Argument, the Argument from Eternal Truths, and the Argument from the Pre-established Harmony.[13] The proof I have in mind might well be termed the *Modal Argument*, for like the Ontological Argument it starts from a definition of God, but establishes His existence not by ordinary but by *modal* reasoning. Let us now examine this argument.[14]

His theory of definition had led to Leibniz' dissatisfaction with the Anselmio-Cartesian Ontological Argument. This theory rests on the classification of definitions as *real* and *nominal: nominal* if not real, and *real* if the *definiens* is shown to be possible, i.e., consistent.[15] The difficulty with the Ontological Argument, which embarks from the definition of God as *the perfect being,* is that it is open to doubt that such a being is possible, and any maneuvering intended to dispel this doubt by demonstrating the freedom from contradiction of the definition would be of doubtful validity. The Leibnizian argument is consequently prepared to jettison perfection, and to start afresh from a quite different definition of God:

> The Geometers, who are the past masters of the art of reasoning, have realized that in order that proofs based on definitions be valid

---

13 See pp. 172 ff. of Russell's *Critical Exposition,* and cf. J. E. Erdmann, *Geschichte der Philosophie,* II, pp. 168-69.

14 That the argument we are about to consider was preferred by Leibniz over others which he gave at times, and that it is this argument which he regarded as the most cogent was, to my knowledge, first pointed out by J. Iwanicki (*Leibniz et les démonstrations mathématiques de l'existence de Dieu* [Strasbourg: Libraire Universitaire d'Alsace, 1933], p. 207). Leibniz habitually supplemented his discussions of the Anselmio-Cartesian Ontological Argument by some such appendage as: "But even leaving out all mention of the divine perfection or grandeur, one can formulate the argument thus far in a more proper and rigorous fashion as follows . . ." (*Phil.,* IV, p. 359). What follows is the Modal Argument.

15 See, e.g., *Phil.,* IV, p. 450.

one must show, or at least postulate, that the notion comprised in any of the definitions used is possible. . . . The same precaution is necessary in every type of reasoning, and above all in the demonstration due to Anselm, Archbishop of Canterbury (*in libro contra insipientem*), which proves that since God is the greatest or most perfect being, He possesses also that perfection termed *existence,* and that consequently He exists; an argument which was subjected to scrutiny by Saint Thomas and other Scholastics, and which was revived by M. Descartes. Regarding this it must be said that the argument is quite valid, providing that the supremely perfect central characteristic of the divine nature—that its essence contains its existence, i.e., that God exists provided only that He is possible. And thus simply omitting all reference to perfection, one can say: *If the Necessary Being is possible, He exists*—doubtless the most beautiful and important proposition of the doctrine of modalities, since it furnishes a passage from possibility to actuality, and it is here and here alone that *a posse ad esse valet consequentia.*[16]

Thus Leibniz establishes the existence of God by defining Him as the *Necessary Being,*[17] and by invoking modal reasoning to show that such a being exists provided only that its existence is possible. It remains for him to demonstrate that the Necessary Being is possible, which he does by adducing another purported theorem of modal logic:

Those who hold that one can never infer actual existence solely from notions, ideas, definitions, or possible essences . . . deny the possibility of the Necessary Being. . . . But if the Necessary Being or *Ens a se* is impossible, then all of the things which owe their existence to others will be impossible, since they must ultimately stem from the *Ens a se.* Thus no existence at all will be possible. . . . This reasoning leads us to another modal proposition . . . which joined with the previous one (*If the Necessary Being is possible, then He exists*) completes the demonstration. This proposition can be formulated thus: *If the Necessary Being does not exist, neither will anything else.*[18]

It is clear, then, that the entire argument is:

1. If the Necessary Being is not possible, then no existence is possible.
2. If the Necessary Being is possible, then He exists.

16 *Ibid.,* pp. 401-2.
17 "Ens a se," "L'Estre de soy," "Ens necessarium," "L'Estre necessaire," "L'Estre qui doit exister parce qu'il est possible."
18 *Phil.,* IV, pp. 359, 406.

3. Therefore, if the Necessary Being does not exist, then nothing exists.

4. But something exists.

5. Hence the Necessary Being exists.[19]

This is the argument which I have termed Leibniz' Modal Argument for the existence of God. In this proof the divine perfection is left altogether out of the picture, and remains to be put in.

We have seen that the perfection of a substance is the same as its quantity of essence, which determines its potentiality for existence. Since God exists necessarily, His existence being contained in His essence, it follows that God has the highest possible degree of perfection. Moreover, God is not only the *necessary,* but also, in consequence, the *perfect* being. At this point we must draw attention to an equivocation in Leibniz' word *perfection* of which he was perfectly aware. There is, firstly, perfection as a measure of potentiality for existence, which we have already considered, and also perfection as a moral attribute, goodness. Leibniz terms the former *metaphysical,* the latter *moral* perfection, and insists that these must be discriminated.[20] God is perfect in both senses; He possesses the maximum amount of essence, and His acts (the sphere of His activity being the world) are the best possible. But while God's existence, hence His metaphysical perfection, is necessary, His goodness as creator, i.e., moral perfection, is contingent and the result of free choice. "The true reason why these things rather than those exist is to be attributed to the free decrees of the divine will, the first and

---

19 The second is *not,* as Leibniz would have it, true by definition. If, however, we grant Leibniz the right to assume that 2 holds for "the Necessary Being," then, since 3 follows from 1 and 2, and since we can scarcely cavil at 4, it is clear that the burden of proof is borne by the (assuredly dubious) premise 1. It should further be remarked that, as Leibniz gives it, the demonstration is an enthymeme, in which the tacit existential premise 4 lurks. Nevertheless, this at worst undermines the claims that the demonstration of possibility is *a priori,* but does not undermine the existence proof.

20 "And lest any should think of confounding moral perfection or goodness with metaphysical perfection or magnitude (*magnitudine*). . . ." it must be remarked that the latter is quantity of essence or reality, while the former arises when metaphysical perfection is the object of a choosing mind (*Phil.,* VII, pp. 305-6; see also G. Grua, *G. W. Leibniz: Textes inédits* [Paris: Presses Universitaires de France, 1948], p. 393). This distinction of Leibniz' has been almost universally overlooked. But if moral and metaphysical perfection are not discriminated, the distinction between moral and metaphysical necessity also collapses, as has been generally charged.

foremost of which is to act in all respects in the most perfect possible way, as befits the wisest of beings." [21]

Leibniz in fact divides God's characteristics into those which are free (contingent) and those which are necessary:

> From this, then, it becomes clear that the acts of God must be distinguished into the free and the necessitated. Thus, that God loves Himself is necessary, for it follows from the definition of *God*. But that God chooses the most perfect cannot be so demonstrated, for its denial implies no contradiction.[22]

And again,

> One can say in a certain sense that it is necessary . . . that God Himself choose what is best. . . . But *this* necessity is not at all at odds with contingence, it not being that necessary which I call logical, geometric, or metaphysical, whose denial is contradictory.[23]

Until the year 1686, when his mature philosophy took form, Leibniz held a different view, as some brief tracts recently published by Grua reveal. He held that God's acts are *both* necessary and free.

> Since GOD necessarily and yet freely chooses the most perfect, whenever there is one thing better than another, it follows that His freedom is always preserved [in choices] although there never existed and never could exist a case in which there is no reason for choosing one of two equally perfect [essences].[24]

God's choice of the best is necessary, but what is to result from that choice is not, for it is not determined with necessity which of the alternatives is the best.

> Though it is true that it is necessary that God choose the best, still it does not follow that the best is necessary or that which He chooses is necessary, for it is not determined with necessity what is best.[25]

Thus when H. W. B. Joseph writes, "What I should like myself to suggest by way of conclusion is, that the acts of God perhaps ought to have been declared free, but not contingent . . ." [26] he suggests to Leibniz a position he did, at an early point in his career, hold. But it is not surprising that Leibniz abandoned this position, for it

---

21 *Phil.*, VII, pp. 309-10, notes.
22 Grua, *Textes*, I, p. 288.
23 *Phil.*, VI, p. 284.
24 Grua, *Textes*, I, p. 276.
25 *Ibid.*, pp. 305-6.
26 *Lectures on the Philosophy of Leibniz*, p. 188.

is difficult to see how what is best could avoid being determined with necessitation when the substances are conceived *sub ratione possibilitatis*. So we later find Leibniz flatly identifying liberty with "contingence or non-necessity." [27]

---

[27] *Phil.*, VI, p. 296.

six

RELATIONS

The Reducibility of Relations

In his important study of Leibniz' philosophy Bertrand Russell wrote:

> Leibniz is forced, in order to maintain the subject-predicate doctrine to the . . . theory that relations, though veritable, are the work of the mind.[1]

Russell here imputes to Leibniz the thesis that, as he puts it, relations are *"merely* ideal," and then goes on to argue that Leibniz cannot consistently adopt this view:

> As applied to relations, [there is] in Leibniz' case, a special absurdity, namely, that the relational propositions, which God is supposed to know, must be strictly meaningless. The only ground for denying the independent reality of relations is, that propositions must have a subject and a predicate. If this be so, a proposition without a subject and a predicate must be no proposition, and must be destitute of meaning. But it is just such a proposition which, in the case of . . .

---

1 Russell, *A Critical Exposition of the Philosophy of Leibniz* (London: George Allen & Unwin Ltd., 1937), p. 14.

relations between monads, God is supposed to see and believe. God, therefore, [for Leibniz] believes in the truth of what is meaningless.[2]

In this chapter we shall argue that Russell's interpretation of Leibniz' views on relations is mistaken, and that his criticisms of these views are entirely inappropriate.

To begin with, we must introduce a distinction that lies at the basis of all of Leibniz' thinking about relations, although he does not formulate it in the particular terms we shall adopt: the distinction between *reducible* and *irreducible* relations.

We shall say that the relation R obtaining between the objects x and y is reducible if there exist predicates $P_1, P_2, \ldots, P_n$ and $Q_1, Q_2, \ldots, Q_m$ such that 1) all the P's are in fact predicates of x; 2) all the Q's are in fact predicates of y; and 3) the relation R is of such a character that the truth-status of xRy can be determined given the conjunction

$$P_1x \ \& \ P_2x \ \& \ \ldots \ \& \ P_nx \ \& \ Q_1y \ \& \ Q_2y \ \& \ \ldots \ \& \ Q_my$$

It is thus the essential feature of a reducible relation that whether the relation obtains or fails to obtain between two objects is always derivable from a suitable *conjunction* of (purely and simply) predicational statements about the objects.

Let us consider some examples of reducible relations:

1. $xRy = x$ is the same color as y. Clearly, if we know the color of object x and that of object y, we can determine whether xRy (x has the same color as y) or not.

2. $xRy = x$ is a colleague of y. Patently, if it is known what is the profession of the man x and what is the profession of the man y, one can determine whether or not xRy (x is a colleague of y).

3. $xRy = x$ is a resident of y. Again, if it is given that the person x has the property of residing in a given street, and that the town y has the property of containing this street, it is decidable whether or not xRy (x is a resident of y).

These illustrations should suffice both to illustrate the essential character of reducible relations, and to suggest that a great many relations will fall into this category.

It is now necessary to introduce one important qualification. We

---

[2] *Ibid.*, pp. 14-15.

must distinguish between *simple* and intrinsically *relational* predicates, and limit the application of the foregoing considerations to simple predicates, ruling out the relational predicates. By an intrinsically relational predicate, I mean one of the type

$$(\lambda z)zRa = \text{the characteristic of standing in the relation}$$
$$R \text{ to the object } a$$

Clearly if such relational predicates are admitted, we can always trivially determine whether or not xRy by asking if x has $(\lambda z)zRy$, the characteristic of standing in the relation R to the object y. The reason why such relational predicates must be excluded in discussing the reducibility of predicates is simple. If we were to permit them, we would have effected no genuine *reduction* to predicates at all, since the same relation we are trying to reduce figures in the specification of the predicate that is being attributed. The reduction procedure is vitiated by a circularity of exactly the same general type that enters into circular definitions and circular arguments.

In excluding relational predicates from consideration we prevent the question "Are there irreducible relations?" from sinking into the triviality of a uniformly negative answer. It is clear that an affirmative answer is now forthcoming, which can best be shown by an example.

Consider the relation (less than/greater than) among the integers. Clearly, for example, $5 < 7$. But from what properties of 5 and 7 could I deduce this fact? Not from knowing that "the square of 5 is 25" and "the square of 7 is 49" without adding that $25 < 49$, i.e., without introducing $<$ once again into the picture.[3] In sum, it is clear, or clear enough for present purposes, that the relation $<$ among integers is reducible in that its obtaining or not cannot be determined on the basis of an incontestably predicational characterization of the objects involved without involving any circularity. Other examples of irreducible relations are afforded by such spatial relations as "being to the left (or to the right) of."

---

[3] Nor again from knowing that 7 has the property $(\lambda x)(\exists z)(5 + z = x) = $ the characteristic belonging to x when there exists some integer z such that $5 + z = x$, without introducing the qualification that $0 < z$, i.e., without bringing $<$ upon the scene once more.

Leibniz' Doctrine of Relations

Before bringing the foregoing considerations to bear upon the philosophy of Leibniz it is necessary to make another important distinction between

1. *Abstract* objects, such as numbers, colors (and other properties), and geometric shapes, and
2. *Concrete* objects or *substances,* i.e., for Leibniz, the monads constituting this actual world of ours, and the possible substances constituting the possible alternative but unrealized worlds.

The point to be emphasized is that there are, for Leibniz, "substances," *things* that exist actually or possibly, and "abstract objects" that do not and could not play the role of *existents* among the constituents of any possible world.

We are now able to formulate what we regard as Leibniz' fundamental teaching on the subject of relations:

Leibniz' Thesis: All relations that obtain *among individual substances* are reducible.

As we interpret the matter, Leibniz is not saying 1) that statements asserting relations between substances are meaningless, nor is he saying 2) that such statements are uniformly false because there are no intersubstantial relations. What he is saying is simply 3) that the only relations that hold among substances are those that are reducible to and derivable from predications about the respective substances.

For the sake of clarity, let us consider a few further illustrations of the sort of contentions in which this thesis would involve Leibniz.

1. $xRy = x$ is older than y. Leibniz would have to hold that, at a given stage of their history, the physiological make-up of persons x and y is such that, by considering separately the physiological characteristics of each, their respective ages can always be determined. (Leibniz would have been pleased by the discovery of tree-ring dating, and rendered positively gleeful by radio-carbon dating techniques.)
2. $xRy = x$ is the father of y. Leibniz would have to hold that the physical make-up of persons x and y is such that by careful analysis

of their respective physical traits, their kinship relationships can always be determined.[4] (He would have rejoiced over recent discoveries in the field of genetic coding.)

The conceptual character of Leibniz' teaching on the subject of relations now becomes clear. *Pace* Russell, Leibniz' thesis about relations is not a logical thesis at all. He does not hold that relational statements are meaningless, or that all relational statements are false; he does not even hold that all relational statements are reducible to predications. In fact, he does not, as I understand him, put forward any *general* thesis about the logic of relational statements as such.

Leibniz' thesis with respect to relations is in fact not a logical thesis about relations, but a metaphysical thesis about the world, or rather about its constituent substances. According to our understanding of his position, Leibniz' view is that all relations between substances are reducible in the sense of inhering in predications about the substances at issue. This is patently a thesis about the metaphysics of substance; substances are such that none but predicationally derivable relations are realized between them.

It would be an analogue to Leibniz' thesis to hold on metaphysical grounds that "all snowflakes are hexagonal" or "all raindrops are spherical." These theses make no contentions about geometric shapes as such, but only about those that, in a given context, are realized by a certain mode of concrete exemplification. Leibniz' thesis, "That substances are such that their only relations are reducible," is analogous in status to the thesis, "That snowflakes are such that their shape is hexagonal." It is not the abstract *logic* of relations (or of shapes) that is at issue, but the physics and metaphysics of substances (or of snowflakes).

The Foundation of "Leibniz' Thesis on Relations"

A word must be said about the ultimate grounds upon which Leibniz' thesis rests. It is, briefly, that substances are completely

---

4 "Thus I hold, as regards relations, that paternity in David is one thing and filiation in Solomon another, but the relation common to both is a mere mental thing, of which *the modifications of singulars are the foundation*" (*Phil.*, II, p. 486; my italics).

defined (prior to their existence, when they only subsist *sub ratione possibilitatis*) by what Leibniz calls their complete individual notions. Two substances, *a* and *b*, are defined through their predicates:

a. $A_1, A_2, A_3, \ldots$
b. $B_1, B_2, B_3, \ldots$

In view of the *completeness* of their individual notions, all truths about *a* must be extractable from the A_i list, and the same holds true of any other substance. In consequence, whenever *a* is in some way related to *b*, so that *aRb* is true, this fact must be extractable from the A_i list. Relations not so extractable cannot, according to Leibniz' thesis, possibly characterize substances, and this, in the final analysis, is a fact, not about relations, but about substances.

The merit of a substance in qualifying for actual realization must belong to it individually and cannot be earned contextually, through its relationship with other substances—even as a wicked parent gains no merit through a good offspring. (This in the final analysis is an ethical thesis, or one belonging to the metaphysics of existential desert.) Only if all the characteristics of substances proceed from their individuality in isolation are the conditions fulfilled that are requisite for judgments of merit involved in divine selection of the possible substances that are to populate the actual world, i.e., the best of all possible worlds.[5]

Leibniz, then, does not teach that relational statements are meaningless, or that intersubstantial relations do not exist, but that all relations that can obtain between substances must derive from their predicates. Relations are "the work of the mind" (in Russell's phrase) because, when substances are under discussion, relational statements are never "ultimate facts," they are always derivative consequences—"confused" consequences, as Leibniz has it—of conjunctions of predications. For Leibniz, relational statements about substances can never afford information about them that is not given more fully and adequately by a complex of predications.

---

5 One must reverse Russell's view. Here the situation is not that Leibniz' metaphysics roots in logic but that his logical doctrine (*praedicatum inest subjecto*) roots in metaphysics.

Such relational statements are true precisely when they are well founded in the properties of the substances at issue.[6]

Critique of Russell's Criticisms

We are now in a position to reappraise Russell's criticisms. Consider first his objections about God's knowledge of relational statements: "Does God know about the intersubstantial relations?" *Yes and no! Yes:* He knows the predicational facts on which such relations must rest because He knows all genuine facts. *Yes:* He knows that some substances relate others in their perceptions because this is represented in their own predicates. *No:* He does not know relational facts "from within," i.e., confusedly without explicit awareness of their predicational basis.

Think of recent discussions of the question, "Can God know what is happening now?" He can know what is happening at 3:30 P.M. on Friday, May 3, 1965, or what is happening contemporaneously with my making of this gesture, but He cannot differentiate one "now" from another—to know what occurs in time from the relational perspective of one positioned within the framework. God cannot know temporal facts from the dis-vantage point of one located *within* the framework. He could never entertain the statement, "It is now 3:30 P.M. Friday, May 3, 1965"; but that does not mean that there are any temporal facts, relating to the events or occurrences that go on in time, that God does not know.

Russell is thus wrong in saying that, in Leibniz' view, God cannot possibly know relational propositions. He does know them, because he knows the predicational facts upon which, in Leibniz' view, all true relational propositions must rest. God's information about substances includes His knowing the complete conjunction of all their predicates. Precisely because all relational facts about substances are reducible to predications, God lacks no information

---

[6] We have been dealing throughout this chapter with relations between *substances* (monadic relations). Relations among (well founded) phenomena are of course also held to be reducible by Leibniz, doubly so because they reduce to inter-monadic relations which then, in turn, come to be grounded in the properties of the several substances involved. Some interesting observations on phenomenal relations occur in the *New Essays*, Bk. II, Chap. xi, §§4 ff.

that true relational statements could conceivably convey. He does not, to be sure, think relationally; He simply conjoins predicates. But He loses nothing by this since there are, in Leibniz' view, no irreducible relational facts about substances for Him to miss. To say that He misses the confused informational perspective of the limited substances is like saying that He lacks information about intoxication because He does not drink.

I come, finally, to the most serious of the confusions present in Russell's criticism of Leibniz: his charge that for Leibniz, as an adherent to subject-predicate logic, every proposition without a subject and a predicate "must be no proposition, and must be destitute of meaning." This is clearly a gross blunder. Even the most rigid subject-predicate logician is willing to countenance statements of the type, "The sugar is white *and* the salt is white," "The grass is dry *or* the grass is wet"—complex statements in which predicational statements are conjoined, disjoined, or otherwise linked by syncategorematic terms. The subject-predicate logician need not (and Leibniz does not) claim a relational statement as meaningless because there is no way of reformulating it as a solitary subject-predicate statement. He can, exactly as Leibniz, regard such statements as synopses of *conjunctions* of predication-statements. Of course Leibniz will grant Russell that "there are (meaningful) propositions which do not have a subject and a predicate," but without abandoning his commitment to the subject-predicate prototype. He takes the position that, in the particular case of propositions about the things of this world, such complex propositions must be capable of being extracted from subject-predicate statements duly *combined* by means of syncategorematic terms.[7]

A Difficulty

There is a serious difficulty in Leibniz' relation-reducibility thesis, one not inherent in the thesis itself, but arising out of a

---

[7] This position of Leibniz', after all, is not far removed from that which was put forward some years after the appearance of Russell's book on Leibniz in the *Tractatus Logico-Philosophicus* (London: Routledge & Kegan Paul, 1933) of Russell's own pupil, Ludwig Wittgenstein. And we may recall that in his introduction to that work Russell emphasized that the teachings of that book were such "that I cannot see any point on which it is wrong."

conflict with other Leibnizian doctrines. As long as Leibniz' thesis is operative, *no two possible substances can be incompossible.* Consider two possible substances defined via their complete individual notions:

    a. $A_1, A_2, A_3, \ldots$
    b. $B_1, B_2, B_3, \ldots$

How can an incompatibility arise? Clearly only if we can extract from the conjunction $A_1(a)$ & $A_2(a)$ & $A_3(a)$ & . . . the fact that "There is no substance x such that $B_1(x)$ & $B_2(x)$ & $B_3(x)$ & . . . ." But this conclusion can follow from the $A_1(a)$ conjunction only if this conjunction gives information about a substance distinct from *a,* information of a kind that irreducibly involves an essential reference to substances distinct from *a,* and thus not genuinely reducible to orthodoxly nonrelational predications about *a.*

It might be thought that one possible exit from this difficulty would be to load into the complete individual notion of a substance a predicate to represent a property of the type "I am a member of possible world #5872," that is, some sort of identifying index for possible-world membership. This would assure, supposing different possible worlds to have different indices, the possibility of inconsistencies. The criticism of this course, which seems to me decisive, is that such a property is not a genuine, qualitative property, but an inherently and ineradicably relational one.

It thus appears that his thesis creates a serious difficulty for the system of Leibniz at another, crucially important, point: the conception of possible worlds not sorted into mutually exclusive alternatives on the basis of considerations of logical compossibility. It is clear that only genuinely relational properties—properties not representable by genuine predicates—can underwrite the incompatibility of alternatively possible substances.

seven

WELL FOUNDING AND
MONADIC AGGREGATION

The Concept of "Well founding" and
Its Role in Leibniz' System

With a metaphysical system such as Leibniz', as with any scientific account of the world by a process of explanatory "reduction" to some ultimate type of thing that is not in common experience, e.g., atoms, force, or energy, the question of explanatory adequacy arises. The factor (or factors) held by the theory to be "ultimately real" must, somehow, give rise to all there is.[1] The instrumentality through which Leibniz achieves this objective is his concept of *well founding*. It is his rule (which he nowhere to my knowledge formulated in the abstract, but constantly applied) that the objects with which one deals in the sciences and the phenomena which

---

[1] Leibniz himself draws this analogy between his own position and that of the atomists (*Phil.,* II, p. 252).

confront one in everyday life result from properties of the monads that constitute larger-scale aggregates. This principle of well founding can be said to assert that all characteristics of the phenomena are well founded in the monadic realm in the sense of being strictly *derivative* from monadic characteristics.

The philosophical importance of this principle lies on the surface—it represents the effort of a philosophy which separates the world into appearance and reality to achieve genuine unity between these disparate elements. Any such philosophy must face the question: How does reality give rise to the appearances? Leibniz' concept of well founding embodies the claim that the theory of monads must face this question, and can deal successfully with it.

Phenomena: Mere *versus* Well Founded

For Leibniz, a *phenomenon* arises when something *appears to* a monad so that it is "represented" in its perceptions. If the condition of things thus to be found in the monad's state corresponds to the conditions actually obtaining in "the external world," i.e., the remaining system of monads, the phenomenon is said to be well founded; when not, the phenomenon is a "mere phenomenon" without an adequate basis in the monadic realm, and therefore an idiosyncratic illusion or delusion. The class of all phenomena is not, for Leibniz, a "night in which all cows are black." Leibniz is perfectly prepared to draw, wholly *within* the "phenomenal" sphere, the familiar, common-sense distinction between the real and the imaginary (much as we might distinguish within the perceptual sphere between genuine oasis-sightings and mere mirages).[2]

---

2 See especially the essay *De modo distinguendi phaenomena realia ab imaginariis* (*Phil.*, VII, pp. 319-22). It is important to realize that the various criteria Leibniz lays down here for the recognition of phenomena as real (well founded), e.g., their vividness and their congruity with the generally observed course of things, represent signs or marks of well foundedness, not its essence. The fact that these marks that are purely "internal" to the realm of observation attach to phenomena that are also well founded in the objective, monadic realm, turn on the pre-established harmony and the fact that this is the best of possible worlds. In effect we are thrown back upon the Cartesian concept that "God is no deceiver."

Monadic Aggregates: The Basis of Real Phenomena

In the system of Leibniz, the monad is the building-block of the universe. Exactly as in the classical atomic theory that all things of the world about us result from the collecting together of huge multiplicities of atoms, so, according to Leibniz, they result from the aggregation of infinities of monads. But how do monads unite into aggregates? The answer is that, in general, they do not unite at all. There are two types of monadic aggregates, "mere aggregates" and "real unities," and most aggregates found *in rerum natura* are of the *mere* variety. A mere aggregate—a stone, for example, or a knife—is comprised of a collection of monads whose "perceptions"' of one another's instantaneous states exhibit a certain degree of mutual similarity and concordance. By virtue of this similarity in points of view, the entities involved appear, to each other and to others, as a unified whole; when one end of the stone moves, so does the rest. Yet they are in actuality unified only accidentally without any pervasive principle of unification. They are united more in the way grains of sand unite into a beach than in the way organs unite into a man's body, their mutual linkage and interaction being of a limited and circumscribed variety.

Given Leibniz' insistence that the only metaphysical realities are monads and their perceptions, it must be asked if the unity of a monadic aggregate, which alone underwrites its reality as a genuine "thing," is purely perceptual, wholly a matter of appearing for others, or has some objective basis. The answer is neither yes nor no. Leibniz makes clear, especially in his important correspondence with Des Bosses, that in the case of organic organisms in general, and *man* pre-eminently, one is not dealing with a "mere aggregate" but an aggregate so intimately unified as to constitute a true unit, a genuinely individuated thing. However, we postpone further discussion of these considerations until we treat of monadic hierarchies in Chapter Nine.

A monadic aggregate is a single "individual thing" only in a remote sense. The aggregate *appears* as one, as a unit, and is thus a phenomenon by virtue of some genuine similarity among its constituents, a feature which gives it some footing in the real, monadic world, and makes it a well founded phenomenon.[3] Such mere aggregates differ from the more highly structurized real unities (to which we shall return in Chapter Nine) in that they do not meet, or come close to meeting, the requirement of the principle of individuation—that of being single substances or at least coming close to them "in all practical purposes." The individuality of an aggregate is really "mental," i.e., perceptual: being apparent only to an internal or external observer, its monadic aggregates are mental entities (*entia mentalia*) which, having a genuine foundation in the monadic realm, are not (like a mirage) simply illusory or delusory phenomena, but *phaenomena bene fundata*.[4]

Causality and Action

Causality is among the most basic well founded phenomena in the metaphysical system of Leibniz. Since each monad is separately "programmed" for the whole of its history, there is no such thing as causal interaction; the only interaction between monads arises in the reciprocal "perception" built into their mutual accord by pre-established harmony. The only thing monads can "do" in relation to one another is to perceive, and to agree (more or less) in their successive states; all talk of causal interaction is purely metaphorical.[5] In the system of Leibniz causality is definable strictly in terms of monadic perception—when two monads come to have a state of agreement that one in whose state this accord is inscribed more sharply, i.e., whose perceptions of the common transaction are clearer, is the active one, and the other the passive one in a strictly figurative "causal interaction." Leibniz writes:

---

3 Unlike a mere phenomenon which exists only in the "perceptions" of the observer without a corresponding foundation within the external realm of other monads. When Leibniz has only phenomena, the next illusory distinction is still preserved by distinguishing between well and ill founded phenomena.

4 The *things* of the sensible world are not the only *phaenomena bene fundata;* they are joined in this category by the perceptual space and time in which they are imbedded, as well as by the "causal" processes by which they seemingly interact.

5 In speaking of "causal interaction" we of course have in mind efficient causality. *Final* causality is another matter altogether; we shall return to it below.

Thus action (or: *activity*) is to be attributed to a monad insofar as it has distinct perceptions, and passivity insofar as its perceptions are confused.[6]

In the correspondence with Arnauld this conception was developed in substantial detail:

> This independence however does not prevent the inter-activity of substances among themselves, for, as all created substances are a continual production of the same sovereign Being according to the same designs and express the same universe or the same phenomena, they agree with one another exactly; and this enables us to say that one acts upon another because the one expresses more distinctly than the other the cause or reason for the changes,—somewhat as we attribute motion rather to a ship than to the whole sea; and this with reason, although, if we should speak abstractly, another hypothesis of motion could be maintained, that is to say, the motion in itself and abstracted from the cause could be considered as something relative. It is thus, it seems to me, that the inter-activities of created substances among themselves must be understood. . . .[7]

It is solely in terms of clearness of perception that efficient causation, itself a phenomenon rather than a monadic reality, comes to be well founded in the monadic realm.

Well Founding and Physics

First we must examine Leibniz' use of some important terms. A characteristic is *primitive* if it characterizes monads, and *derivative* if it characterizes monadic aggregates, that is, if it derives in the aggregation of monads from some primitive monadic characteristic.[8] But what is primitive is simply the series of the perceptions of monads and nothing else. Thus Leibniz comes to call perception *primitive force,* the clear perceptions of a monad and its appetition toward new clear perceptions being its *primitive active force (vis primitiva agendi)* and its confused perceptions *primitive passive force (vis primitiva patiendi)* or, preferably, *prime matter (materia prima).*[9]

---

[6] *Monadology,* §49. Cf. *Phil.,* II, pp. 57, 59, 71, 112, 113; and VII, p. 312.

[7] *Phil.,* II, p. 147. Leibniz utilizes this concept of activity also in the context of voluntary human action: ". . . our voluntary action, however, is always spontaneous, in such a way that its principle is in the agent" (*Causa Dei,* §28; *Phil.,* VI, p. 443).

[8] *Phil.,* II, pp. 251, 306, 517; *Math.,* VI, pp. 101, 236.

[9] *Phil.,* II, pp. 206, 244, 245, 250, 251, 252; *Math.,* VI, pp. 100-1.

As can be expected, these primitive features of monads give rise to derivative aggregational characteristics. From the passive aspect of monads, their prime matter, there arises in aggregation what Leibniz calls "secondary matter" (*materia secunda*)—the "matter" of the physics of his time—along with its principal features, especially the two basic derivative passive forces (*vires derivativae patiendi*): inertia (*resistentia*) and solidity (impenetrability, *antitypia*).[10] There are also several derivative active forces (*vires derivativae agendi*), the "forces" of the physics of the time, including especially what Leibniz terms "live force" (*vis viva*), by which he understands essentially what is now called kinetic energy,[11] and also *conatus* (or *solicitatio*, i.e., "virtual velocity"), whose ultimate foundation lies in monadic appetition. Thus Leibniz holds that the entire subject matter of the physical science of his time (mechanics) is derived from the two primitive forces, since the structure of the monad, its series of perceptions, suffices to account for the fundamental concepts of mechanics.[12]

Leibniz' mechanism enables him to proceed beyond this point, for according to it, all natural processes are complexes of mechanical ones, and thus all natural phenomena (human perception alone excepted) can be explained mechanically. "It is the case that all the phenomena of material objects (*corpora naturalia*), excepting perceptions, can be accounted for in terms of magnitude, shape, and motion." [13] "All the phenomena of material objects (corps) can be explained mechanically or by the corpuscular philosophy, in accordance with certain mechanical principles. . . ." [14] "Moreover in the phenomena, i.e., in the aggregate(s) resulting (from monads), all is explained mechanically. . . ." [15] "Nature must always be explained mechanically and mathematically, provided one bears in

---

[10] *Phil.,* II, pp. 171, 184, 306; *Math.,* VI, pp. 100, 236-37.

[11] Its derivative character is assured by the statement: "The forces which arise from mass and velocity are derivative" (*Phil.,* II, p. 251). Regarding derivative active forces see also *Phil.,* II, pp. 2, 171, 201 ff., 275-76, and *Math.,* VI, pp. 101-3, and 236-37.

[12] For Leibniz' derivation of mechanics see the essay *Specimen dynamicum pro admirandis naturae legibus circa corporum vires et mutuas actiones detegendis et ad suas causas revocandis* (*Math.,* VI, pp. 234 ff.; cf. pp. 98 ff.).

[13] *Phil.,* II, p. 314.

[14] *Ibid.,* p. 78.

[15] *Ibid.,* p. 250. This holds good even in the organic realm, for even organic things are a kind of automaton or natural machine, "which is a machine not only as a whole, but also in the smallest parts" (PNG, §3; *Monadology,* §64).

mind that the principles or laws of mechanics themselves do not derive from mere mathematical extension, but from metaphysical reasons." [16] The mechanical properties of material objects are "derived" directly in aggregation, and their remaining properties are to be accounted for mechanically.

From this viewpoint we also see the intimate connection among Leibniz' metaphysic, his monadism, and his mechanistic position in natural philosophy. By making the derivation of mechanical characteristics suffice for aggregational characteristics in general, Leibniz' mechanism provides the machinery with which he endeavors to show the explanatory adequacy of the monadic theory.[17]

It remains to say a word concerning the relation of Leibniz' theory of well founding to the Principle of Perfection. The connection between them is evidenced by the fact that the rule of well founding is a minimum principle. Well founding is an aspect of perfection because it calls for economy in the machinery of cosmological explanation, holding that the phenomena are *in toto* to be accounted for by means of the metaphysical apparatus of the monadology.

Harmony and Well Founding

What element is there in the structure of the realm of monads that makes it possible for well founded phenomena to arise? Any answer to this question must be provided by the pre-established harmony, which is responsible for any general, inter-monadic structure possessed by the realm of strictly independent monads.

We recall that an aggregate of monads is a (phenomenal) unit as a result of being perceived as such by an external monad; [18] thus phenomena arise in monadic perception. Consequently there are two aspects to a well founded phenomenon, subjective and objective. The subjective aspect is brought to light in considering the perceiving monad itself: the phenomenon is a unit since it is an *ens mentalis* for it. There is also an objective aspect in well founded

---

16 *Phil.*, II, p. 58.
17 This aspect of Leibniz' mechanism is most explicit in his illuminating letter to De Volder (*ibid.*, pp. 248-53).
18 ". . . only monads will be real, but the union will be supplied in the phenomenon by the action (*operatio*) of the perceiving soul" (*ibid.*, p. 435).

phenomena: what is perceived is some feature of an actual aggregation of monads constituting a ground for perception because of
certain similarities of state of its constituent monads. The well
foundedness is thus the objective and the phenomenality the subjective side of the well founded phenomenon. Both of these states of
affairs—the inner accord of the constituents of the aggregate, and
the external accord of aggregate with percipient—prevail in virtue
of the pre-established harmony. It is thus clear how the pre-established harmony, by providing the machinery for well founding,[19]
furnishes the key to the answer to our initial question in regard to
the system of Leibniz.

---

[19] "The explanation of all phenomena solely through the perceptions of monads
functioning in harmony with each other. . . ." (*Phil.*, II, p. 450). See also
the *Système Nouveau* (*Phil.*, IV, pp. 471-77). The pre-established harmony
was termed "the hypothesis of the concomitance or of the accord of substances
between themselves" in the correspondence with Arnauld, a far more suggestive terminology. (*Phil.*, II, pp. 58, 74, etc.)

eight

SPACE AND TIME: MOTION
AND INFINITY

The Basis of Leibniz' Theory of
Space and Time

To put the matter somewhat generally, one can say that the core
of Leibniz' theory of space and time [1] is that these are nothing apart

---

[1] Leibniz' views on this topic are most completely set forth in correspondence
between him and Samuel Clarke during 1715–1716, in the course of which
Leibniz attacked, and Clarke defended, the Newtonian theory of space and
time. (For this latter theory see the first scholium of the *Principia*.) For in-
formation regarding the occasion of this dispute with Clarke, I refer the
reader to Gerhardt's purely historical *Einleitung* to this correspondence (*Phil.*,
VII, pp. 347-51; the correspondence itself is given in *Phil.*, VII, pp. 352-440).
We shall draw very heavily on this correspondence for information regarding
Leibniz' own views, which are there set forth in considerable detail. He had
already contested the Newtonian theory in the *Nouveaux Essais* of 1704 (*Phil.*,
V, p. 141).
  The roots of the Leibnizian theory of space and time are to be sought in
the *Pacidus Philalethi* of 1676 (Couturat, *Opuscules*, pp. 594 ff.). Neverthe-
less the theory was not, as far as I have been able to discover, formulated prior
to 1695. In his objections to the *Système Nouveau* (1695), Foucher writes:
"I do not agree with you, that there is any reason to postulate unities which

from the things "in" them, but owe their existence to the ordering relations that obtain among things. Space and time are thus not pre-existing receptacles which exist independently of and (logically) prior to the existence of the entities which are supposed embedded within them. They are (well founded) *phenomena,* and as such their existence is secondary, since it is derivative from the monads and their properties.

The general character of the process of derivation that Leibniz envisages for space and time is readily pictured. In regard to space, all monads perceive one another at every given temporal juncture, so the entire actual world is (for each of its member monads) one vast monadic aggregate at any given time. For Leibniz, space is this relationship among all the monads inherent in their contemporaneous mutual perceptions, this general universal ordering throughout time (i.e., at any given time). The general order obtaining among the monads of this world in virtue of the pre-established harmony, and thus resting ultimately on the Principle of Perfection, is the basis for the well founding of the phenomenon of space.

The situation is similar with respect to time. The mutual agreement obtaining between monadic states in virtue of the pre-established harmony is such that, to every state of a given monad at some instant of its private time, there corresponds exactly one (contemporaneous) state of every other monad. This correspondence is defined in terms of closeness of similarity. (It might be helpful to draw an analogy with two skew lines in space—to every point on each there corresponds just one point of the other that lies nearest to it.) It is this corresponding state of the other monad, the state most similar to it on the basis of *purely qualitative* comparisons, that is simultaneous (contemporaneous) with it in public, intermonadic time. Time as well as space is derivative from the primitive characteristics of the individual monads.

---

cause the composition and the reality of extension" (*Phil.,* IV, p. 486); for Leibniz had spoken of "unités substantielles" as opposed to mere aggregates (*Phil.,* IV, p. 482). In the remarks on these objections Leibniz writes: "It seems that the author of the objections did not understand correctly my opinion. Extension or space are only relations [resulting] from order, or orders of coexistence" (*Phil.,* IV, p. 491). This is the first formulation of the Leibnizian theory of space and time I have located, but because this theory rests logically on two ingredients—the theory of monads, and the treatment of the problems of infinity and continuity—both of which were ready circa 1686, I should conjecture that it was developed prior to 1695.

The fact that our actual universe has its kind of spatial and temporal structure is, for Leibniz, a contingent feature of the world. If an imperfect deity had created an imperfect world, in which the mutual perceptions of the (independent) monads did not accord neatly, the world might have had a non-continuous space with holes in it, or even have been a chaos with no spatial structure at all. Similarly, if the appetitions of the independent monadic programs did not exhibit the requisite matching and coherence, time (i.e., public, inter-monadic time, in contrast to the private time built into each individual monadic program) would not be in existence.

The Nature of Space and Time

The universal correspondence established by the mutual perceptions of all created individual substances is the result, not of any mutual causal influence, but of a divinely ordained accord, the pre-established harmony.[2] Each substance, however, by no means is represented or perceived by every other substance in an equally sharp and detailed way; each one perceives more clearly those substances closer to, or more important for, it,[3] perceiving the whole universe from its own point of view. Leibniz compares the individual monad to

> a center or point which, though itself simple, is the locus of an infinity of angles formed by the lines which intersect at it.[4]

---

[2] Leibniz is so concerned to show that the accord among contemporaneous substances cannot arise by causal influence because, being a mechanist, he could not admit instantaneous causal influence at a distance. He clearly recognized the causal independence of contemporaries. "If of two elements *which are not simultaneous* one comprehends the cause of the other, the former is considered as preceding, the latter as succeeding," is his definition of temporal order (*Math.*, VII, p. 18; tr. by H. Weil, *Philosophy of Mathematics and Natural Science* [Princeton: Princeton University Press, 1949], p. 101). The theory of relativity has lent interest to this definition. Thus it is via this theory that the definition of events as contemporaries if neither is causally connected with the other is incorporated into Whitehead's "philosophy of organism" (cf. *Process and Reality* [Cambridge: Cambridge University Press, 1929], p. 95). Thus, strangely enough, it is in order to uphold a physical theory of causation— mechanism—that Leibniz is driven to that total denial of causation at the metaphysical level which is formulated in the pre-established harmony.

[3] For the principles governing the clarity of perception see *Phil.*, II, p. 90, and *Monadology*, §60.

[4] PNG, §2; cf. §11.

It is thus that the monad combines infinite qualitative (perceptual) richness with absolute simplicity (*spatial,* i.e., structural).

Against Leibniz' theory of space as a well founded phenomenon, Russell objects [5] that Leibniz cannot regard space as purely phenomenal and subjective and also maintain that, as he puts it, "the perceptions of different monads differ, owing to the difference of their points of view." The objection, though correct, is not damaging to Leibniz, and not wholly fair to him. The essentials of his position are clear: the monads and their states (perceptions) are basic. These perceptions are coordinated (in the pre-established harmony) to give rise to a system of mutually accommodating points of view. Space as a well founded phenomenon results from this system of coordinated perceptions.

At no two different moments of time can an individual substance have the same state, for if its state were exactly the same, the whole system of its contemporary substance states would have to be the same, and therefore, moments of time being defined in terms of contemporary substance states, the moments of time would also be the same. Thus each individual substance is subject to a perpetual, continuous change of state, the only activity of which it is capable.[6] Leibniz chooses to call it appetition but connotations of this term toward some sort of active, conscious, seeking or striving must be avoided.

From the very first Leibniz presented the monad as a *continuant,* a perduring substance persisting through change; [7] in mathematical jargon a one-parameter family of states is involved,[8] the history of the monad being given in terms of an ordered "genidentity-class" of monadic states. This change of state of a substance (appetition) is temporally continuous, and at any instant every monad represents the entire universe from its own point of view with varying

---

[5] Russell, *Critical Exposition,* p. 122.

[6] We have not spoken of "force" as associated with individual substances, nor made much of "Leibniz' dynamism." This is because "force" in the philosophy of Leibniz is a derived notion, resulting from perceptions and their changes. As to dynamism, or the doctrine of unextended centers of force, this ill describes Leibniz' theory of substance, for his individual substances are, as we shall see, a good deal more.

[7] *Disc. de Metaph.,* corresp. with Arnauld, RMM.

[8] "A complete or perfect singular substance involves all its predicates, past, present, and future" (Couturat, *Opuscules,* p. 520).

degrees of clarity,[9] making for the continuous distribution of monads in space. Space, like time, is a structure of relations of an appropriate sort.

Space, according to Leibniz, is an *ordering of coexisting things,* but what are the *things* at issue? Two alternative answers, both perfectly proper, can be given. Taking the things as monads, we arrive at real, metaphysical space; taking them as aggregates, as phenomena, we arrive at the phenomenal space with which one deals in ordinary life and in the sciences. It should also be noted that the important role of the term *coexisting* in Leibniz' definition of space subordinates this concept to that of time and temporal considerations.

Time, too, has a dual nature for Leibniz. There is the essentially private, intra-monadic time of each individual substance continuing, by appetition, through its transitions from state to state. There is also the public time obtaining throughout the system of monads in general, made possible by the inter-monadic correlations established by the pre-established harmony. Leibniz' standard definition of time as *the order of non-contemporaneous things* [10] would be vitiated by an obvious circularity if it did not embody a distinction between intra- and inter-monadic time, carrying the latter back to (i.e., well founding it within) the former.

The monads are ordered with respect to their point of view; it is always possible to find a monad differing from a given monad in point of view by less than any preassigned difference. This is basic to both the Leibnizian theory of space and to his denial of a vacuum in nature. The monads are also continuously ordered with regard to structure. As Russell puts it, "If two substances differ by a finite difference there must be . . . a continuous series of intermediate substances, each of which differs infinitesimally from the next." [11] In this way Leibniz denies what he terms a "vacuum of kinds" (*vacuum formarum*).[12]

It follows from these considerations concerning monads that physical space is a plenum.[13] Moreover, all the processes of the

9 "All singular created substances are diverse expressions of the same universe, . . . but the expressions vary in perfection" (Couturat, *Opuscules,* p. 521).
10 *Math.,* VII, p. 18.
11 Russell, *Critical Exposition,* pp. 64-65. Cf. Buchenau-Cassirer, II, p. 558.
12 *Phil.,* II, p. 168; *Phil.,* VI, p. 548; *Nouveaux Essais,* III, Chap. 4, §13.
13 Cf. *Monadology,* §§66-69.

physical world, e.g., motion or impact, take place continuously, according to Leibniz.[14] The principle of continuity as applied to the physical world, Leibniz' extension of the classical principle *natura non facit saltus,* is put to work by him throughout the physical and metaphysical domains.

Space and Time: Some Polemical Issues

Leibniz' central argument against the independent reality of space and time is that this would violate the Principle of Sufficient Reason. The following is a good formulation of this argument:

> Space is something absolutely uniform; and, without the things placed in it, one point of space does not absolutely differ in any respect whatsoever from another point of space. Now from hence it follows, (supposing space to be something in itself, besides the order of bodies among themselves,) that 'tis impossible there should be a reason, why God, preserving the same situations of bodies among themselves, should have placed them in space after one certain particular manner, and not otherwise; why every thing was not placed the quite contrary way, for instance, by changing East into West.[15]

Absolute time would similarly violate the Principle of Sufficient Reason, and is therefore impossible.[16] The independence of time would further violate the Principle of Perfection, for, if this were possible, God might have created the world sooner, thus increasing the amount of existence, and hence of perfection.[17]

These arguments are not solely intended to refute the absoluteness of space and time, but additionally to dispense with the substantiality of spatial extension as conceived of by the Cartesians. Leibniz held that the Cartesians erred in regarding spatiality as

---

14 See, for example, the discussion of motion in the *Dynamica, Math.,* VI, pp. 320-26.

15 *Phil.,* VII, p. 364 (3d letter to Clarke, §5).

16 "Supposing any one should ask, why God did not create every thing a year sooner; . . . if time was any thing distinct from things existing in time. For it would be impossible there should be any reason, why things should be applied to such particular instants, rather than to others, their succession continuing the same" (*Phil.,* VII, p. 364). Cf. the argument of Parmenides (fragment no. 8) against the createdness of the existent that "if it came from nothing, what need could have made it arise rather later than sooner?"

17 *Phil.,* VII, p. 405 (5th letter to Clarke, §56).

pertaining to substances, for he regarded extension not as something primitive, but as derived from substances. The concept of substance which gives rise to the monad is simply inapplicable to space. Leibniz also has an *argumentum ad hominem* against the Cartesian position. He argues that spatial extension is nothing privileged, and that if it gives rise to substance, so ought temporal extension.[18]

There are three aspects of the theory of space of Newton, as defended by Clarke, which Leibniz is especially concerned to refute—the absoluteness of space, the existence of a void, and the thesis that space is the sensorium of God. Leibniz also wishes to refute the suggestion made by Clarke in his third letter that space is some sort of property.

Leibniz' refutation of absolute space, based on the argument that this involves a violation of the Principle of Sufficient Reason, we have considered already. The impossibility of a void is shown by arguing that a void would be a special case of an absolute space:

> The same reason, which shows that extramundane space is imaginary, proves that all empty space is an imaginary thing; for they differ only as greater and less.[19]

The position that space is the sensorium of God is met by Leibniz on theological grounds, for if this were so, space would be an entity wholly outside of God's power, and He would be dependent upon it.[20]

Next we come to Leibniz' arguments against the thesis that space is a property or attribute. If this were true it would have to belong to some substance, but then what of void space?[21] If space *is not* regarded as an attribute of God it would be completely beyond his power, and there would be an infinity of eternal things beside

---

[18] "To conceive of extension as something absolute arises from this source, that we conceive of space as a sort of substance, whereas it is no more a substance than is time" (*Phil.*, II, p. 510).

[19] *Phil.*, VII, p. 372 (4th letter to Clarke, §7).

[20] "God cannot destroy it, nor even change it in any respect" (*Phil.*, VII, p. 373; 4th letter to Clarke, §10). To hold that space is the *sensorium* of God involves Clarke in theological difficulties, for what need can an omniscient being, who has *a priori* knowledge of all, have of an organ of sensation? Leibniz meets Clarke's efforts at explanation with frigid sarcasm: "I find, in express words, in the Appendix to Sir Isaac Newton's *Opticks,* that space is the *sensorium* of God. But the word *sensorium* hath always signified the organ of sensation. He, and his friends, may now, if they think fit, explain themselves quite otherwise: I shall not be against it" (*Phil.*, VII, p. 356; 2d letter to Clarke, §3).

[21] *Phil.*, VII, p. 372 (4th letter to Clarke, §8).

God; [22] if it *is* a property of God, "It does not appear reasonable to say, that this empty space, either round or square, is a property of God." [23] Further, "a property of God must (which is very strange) be made up of the affections of creatures; for all finite spaces, taken together, make up infinite space." [24] If space is regarded as a property of the things which occupy it, then the distinction between space and place breaks down,[25] and so Leibniz feels that he has completely disposed of the thesis that space is a property.

So far we have dealt almost solely with the negative and polemical portions of Leibniz' theory of space and time. Let us now consider the positive part of that theory. As indicated already, Leibniz' oft-stated position is that space and time are orders of things, and not things. He uses as example the relationships of a family tree,[26] and adduces another example of order or relation which, although it is somewhat lengthy, I give *in extenso* because it throws much light on the logical foundations of Leibniz' philosophy:

> The ratio or proportion between two lines L and M, may be con-
> ceived three several ways; as a ratio of the greater L, to the lesser M;
> as a ratio of the lesser M, to the greater L; and lastly, as something
> abstracted from both, that is, as the ratio between L and M, without
> considering which is the antecedent, or which the consequent; which
> the subject, and which the object. And thus it is, that proportions
> are considered in music. In the first way of considering them, L the
> greater; in the second, M the lesser, is the subject of that accident,
> which philosophers call relation. But, which of them will be the sub-

22 *Phil.*, VII, p. 373 (4th letter to Clarke, §10).

23 *Phil.*, VII, p. 398 (5th letter to Clarke, §38).

24 *Phil.*, VII, p. 398 (5th letter to Clarke, §40). Note that Leibniz' arguments are theological based on the traditional conception of God. Leibniz here deploys his forces with considerable skill. Remark the element of raillery in the following passage: "God's immensity makes him actually present in all spaces. But now if God is in space, how can it be said that space is in God, or that it is a property of God? We have often heard that a property is in its subject; but we never heard, that a subject is in its property" (*Phil.*, VII, p. 399; 5th letter to Clarke, §45).

25 This argument appears from the following two passages: "The space taken up by a body, will be the extension of that body. Which is an absurdity; since a body can change space but cannot leave its extension" (*Phil.*, VII, p. 398; 5th letter to Clarke, §37). "Everything has its own extension, its own duration; but it has not its own time, and does not keep its own space" (*Phil.*, VII, p. 399; 5th letter to Clarke, §46). Further, Leibniz argues that to regard the spatial position of a thing as its property is to commit a rhetorical blunder: "But this is a strange property or affection, which passes from one subject to another" (*Phil.*, VII, p. 398; 5th letter to Clarke, §39).

26 *Phil.*, VII, p. 401 (5th letter to Clarke, §47).

ject, in the third way of considering them? It cannot be said that both of them, L and M together, are the subject of such an accident; [27] for if so, we should have an accident in two subjects, with one leg in one, and the other in the other; which is contrary to the notion of accidents. Therefore we must say, that this relation, in this third way of considering it, is indeed out of the subjects; but being neither a substance, nor an accident, it must be a mere ideal thing, the consideration of which is nevertheless useful.[28]

Here the basis of Leibniz' denial of reality to space and time is brought fully to light. They are relational, as is clearly and succinctly revealed by the above passage. Though he is willing to recognize the logical value of relations, and often praises Jungius for securing their position in logic, Leibniz has a firm prejudice in metaphysics in favor of subject-predicate logic. This prejudice has repercussions throughout Leibniz' philosophy, and his theories of space and time are among the best examples.

In his fifth letter to Clarke, Leibniz gives his answer to the psychological question of the origin of the notion of space.[29] It is essentially that the *place* of an object is its relation to a number of other objects whose relations to each other are not changed, and *space* is "that which results from all places taken together." [30] This ordering of positions relates not *abstracta* but *substances*:

> Now simple substance, although it does not in itself have extension, nevertheless has position, which is the ground of extension, since extension is the continuous simultaneous repetition of position—as we say a line is made by the fluxion of a point. . . .[31]

Space and time are ideal, or rather are phenomena,[32] space because it is nothing but the order or relation of (simultaneous) existents, and time since it is relational, and involves the labyrinth of

---

[27] This is exactly what is now sometimes done in logic in defining a relation as a class of ordered pairs. If this is done the subject of the relational statement is the ordered pair and the predicate the assertion of class membership.

[28] *Phil.*, VII, p. 401 (5th letter to Clarke, §47).

[29] *Ibid.*

[30] *Ibid.*

[31] *Phil.*, II, p. 339.

[32] Though Leibniz used both terms there is no conflict. As they arise in the real world space and time are phenomena. As objects of mathematics, "en soy" or apart from the order of real things, they are ideal (*Phil.*, VII, p. 396; 5th letter to Clarke, §33).

the continuum.[33] However, space and time are not chimera but well founded phenomena, *phaenomena bene fundata*. There arises the question of what monadic properties and characteristics provide the *fundamenta* for space and time.

Let us first consider space. How is the difference in relation or position grounded within the monad? In the internal composition of every monad is reflected its relations to all others. We are once more brought back to the pre-established harmony, which sees to it that each monad mirrors the universe from its own point of view. This alone is the *fundamentum* of space. Time is grounded in the change of state, the appetition, of the monads, for Leibniz defines temporal order in terms of monadic states:

> If of two elements which are not simultaneous one comprehends the ground (*ratio*) of the other the former is considered as preceding, the latter as succeeding.[34]

The space and time we have been considering are those to which the monads, the actual substances, belong; this space and time are manifolds of order among the monads with respect to coexistence and succession, respectively.[35] This is the fashion in which space and time are conceived of in the correspondence with Clarke. However, at times, Leibniz takes two other different points of view.

1. At times Leibniz has in mind *mathematical* space and time. This is the space of which he speaks in *Phil.*, IV, p. 394, giving it as an example of a continuum where the parts may be assumed in any way, and which is consequently not real, but ideal.

---

33 "Nothing of time does ever exist, but instants; and an instant is not even itself a part of time. Whoever considers these observations, will easily apprehend that time can only be an ideal thing" (*Phil.*, VII, p. 402; 5th letter to Clarke, §49).

34 *Math.*, VII, p. 18.

35 "God not only perceives the individual monads and their modifications, but also their relations—and in just this resides their reality. Primary among these (relations) is duration, i.e., the order of successives, and position, i.e., the order of coexistence (*Phil.*, II, p. 438). The space and time of our perception is a confused, aggregational, version of the space and time seen by God. However, even the latter is phenomenal. It is, furthermore, important to remark that space and time are not, strictly speaking, orders of existents or substances, but orders of created *existents*. God is outside both space and time: "Space is not the place of all things; for it is not the place of God. Otherwise there would be a thing coeternal with God, and independent upon Him; nay, he Himself would depend upon it, if He has need of place" (*Phil.*, VII, p. 409; 5th letter to Clarke, §79).

2. Sometimes space and time are conceived of as ordering manifolds not only among the actual substances, but among all possible substances. This is the space of which Leibniz says: "It is a relation, an ordering, not solely between the existents, but also among the possibles as though they existed." [36] In this passage it seems that space is one huge system in which all the possible worlds are located. In still other passages Leibniz inclines to the view, inconsistent with his philosophy, of one spatio-temporal receptacle into which any one of the possible worlds could have been put.

> And therefore, one must not say, as the author does here, that God created things in what particular space, and at what particular time he pleased. For, all time and all spaces being in themselves perfectly uniform and indiscernible from each other, one of them cannot please more than another.[37]

The spaces here discussed, which exist independently of the actual world, exist only in the mind of God, since this is where the possible worlds have their being.[38] It is like the chessboard when the players play mentally or blindfolded.[39]

These are two of Leibniz' variant conceptions of space and time. However, as is clear from what has already been said, he generally takes space and time to be orders among the actual substances, the monads.

We have seen the basis of the Leibnizian theory of space and time, whence arises the thesis that space and time are well founded phenomena, and how it is implemented. This does not exhaust the content of Leibniz' pronouncements on this subject. We will next consider some of these further views.

1. *The Dimensionality of Space.* Leibniz defends a position which at first seems inconsistent with other parts of his theory of space. He holds that tri-dimensionality of space is *necessary,* even though space itself is but the order of contingents. To Clarke he objects that absolute space is a limitation on God, and yet insists on the absoluteness of its dimensions.

---

[36] *Phil.,* V, p. 136. Cf. *"pro loci seu ordinis possibilis existendi"* (*Phil.,* VII, p. 304).

[37] *Phil.,* VII, p. 406 (5th letter to Clarke, §60). Cf. *Phil.,* VII, pp. 303-4, and *Phil.,* III, p. 400.

[38] "But if there were no creatures, space and time would be only in the ideas of God" (*Phil.,* VII, pp. 376-77; 4th letter to Clarke, §41).

[39] See *Phil.,* V, p. 136.

But with the dimensions of matter it is not thus: the ternary number is determined for it not by the reason of the best, but by a geometrical necessity, because the geometricians have been able to prove that there are only three straight lines perpendicular to one another which can intersect at one and the same point.[40] Nothing more appropriate could have been chosen to show the difference there is between the moral necessity that accounts for the choice of wisdom and the brute necessity of Strato and the adherents of Spinoza, who deny to God understanding and will, than a consideration of the difference existing between the reason for the laws of motion and the reason for the ternary number of the dimensions: for the first lies in the choice of the best and the second in a geometrical and blind necessity.[41]

However, the reasons motivating Leibniz to take this position are brought to light in the correspondence with Clarke.[42] The dimensionality of space must be determined by an absolute necessity, for if more dimensions had been possible, God could have created a somehow "bigger" universe.

2. *The Measurability of Space and Time.* To Clarke's objection, "that Space and Time are quantities, which Situation and Order are not," [43] Leibniz replies:

Relative things have their quantity, as well as absolute ones. For instance, ratios or proportions in mathematics, have their quantity, and are measured by logarithms; and yet they are relations. And therefore though time and space consist in relations, yet they have their quantity.[44]

The amount of time between two moments is an exact measure of the number of states of the universe intermediate between them. Into a given amount of time only a certain fixed number of distinct states of the universe can be put, neither more nor less. The amount of time is an exact measure of temporal order, and this can only be altered by adding or dropping some states which, with the actual state of affairs, is impossible.[45] This gets Leibniz around

---

40 Clearly this argument is circular.
41 *Phil.*, VI, p. 323; *Theodicy*, §351; cf. *Phil.*, III, p. 419.
42 See Clarke's 4th letter, and Leibniz' 5th.
43 *Phil.*, VII, p. 384.
44 *Phil.*, VII, p. 404 (5th letter to Clarke, §54).
45 In his 4th letter, Clarke objects "that Time is not merely the Order of things succeeding each other . . . because the Quantity of Time may be greater or less, and yet that Order continue the same" (*Phil.*, VII, p. 387). To this Leibniz' reply is: "For if the time is greater, there will be more successive and like

the difficulty that an order-preserving one-one correspondence is possible between line-segments of different lengths.[46] The measurability of both spatial and temporal relations rests on the fact that:

> In both these orders—time and space—we can speak of *propinquity* or *remoteness* of the elements according as *fewer or more connecting links are required to discern their mutual order.* Two points, then, are nearer to one another when the points between them and the structure arising out of them with maximal definiteness, present something relatively simpler.[47]

It is interesting to note that in a passage of the *Nouveaux Essais* Leibniz asserts the possibility of a changeless duration, an "empty" time.[48] In this respect time is unlike space in which no void is possible. A void in space would be measurable, but a void in time would be of indeterminate length, and whoever maintained that it was of length zero, i.e., had no duration at all, could not be refuted.[49] Thus a "durée sans changemens" is possible because its actualization would make no difference. However, arguing strictly from the Principle of the Identity of Indiscernibles, Leibniz ought to have taken a more positive stand. He should have maintained that a temporal vacuum is just as impossible as a spatial one.

3. *Space and Analysis Situs.* Against Leibniz' theory of space the objection of strangeness may be brought, though perhaps by now it is sufficiently clear that such an objection is valid neither in science nor in philosophy. Leibniz' space is a space of real points (i.e., monads) without real lines, planes, or solids; it is a space where one can tell—if one is God—whether two monad-points are close together (for then their points of view will be similar), and

---

states interposed; and if it be less, there will be fewer; seeing there is no vacuum, nor condensation, or penetration, (if I may so speak), in times, any more than in places" (*Phil.,* VII, p. 415; 5th letter to Clarke, §105).

[46] See Couturat, *Opuscules,* p. 610.

[47] *Math.,* VII, p. 18.

[48] *Phil.,* V, p. 142. (Bk. I, Chap. 15, §11).

[49] I quote the most important parts of the passage cited in n. 48: "If there were a void in time, i.e., a duration without any change, it would be impossible to determine its length. . . . But one would [then] not be able to refute someone who might say that two successive worlds touch as to duration, so that one begins necessarily when the other ends, without any [intermediate] interval being possible. One would not be able to refute him, I say, because this interval is undeterminable."

yet it is meaningless to ask for the distance between them, for distance, being a relation, has no place in the monadic realm.

Such a world must have seemed weird a century ago, but these spaces, termed *topological* spaces, are the common familiar property of mathematicians today. Topology is a branch of mathematics that has received much attention of late. In the last century it was called *analysis situs;* fittingly enough, its founder was Leibniz.[50] But it must not be forgotten that Leibniz' theory of space is a good theory held for bad reasons, for it stems, in large measure, from prejudice in favor of the subject-predicate logic.

4. *The Non-Homogeneity of Time.* There is a total lack of homogeneity in time, according to Leibniz. He holds that it is not only impossible that the state of the universe is the same at two different instants, but even that every earlier state of the universe has a logical, or natural, priority over every later state.[51] Precisely what it is that Leibniz has in mind one can only conjecture. I should suggest that this priority is a consequence of continuity considerations. An earlier instant cannot be interchanged with a later one because this would involve a break in the continuity of the development of the universe.

Motion

In the dialogue *Pacidus Philalethi* of 1676, in which some of the major doctrines of Leibniz' later philosophy are adumbrated, he adheres to an interesting theory of motion, that of transcreation.[52] He writes that motion

cannot, I think, be better explained than when we say that the body

---

50 The reader is referred to the opuscule *De analysis situs (Math.*, V, pp. 179-83), and to Chap. 9, "Le Calcul Géométrique," of Couturat, *Logique.* The Leibnizian space is termed an "Umgebungsraum," a "neighborhood-space." (See Seiffert and Threlfall, *Lehrbuch der Topologie* [New York: Chelsea Publishing Company, 1947], chap. 2, #5; or Alexandroff and Hopf, *Topologie* [Berlin: J. Springer, 1935], p. 30.)

51 "I admit, however, that there is this difference between instants and points— one point of the universe has no advantage of priority over another, while a preceding instant always has the advantage of priority, not merely in time but in nature, over following instants" (*Phil.*, III, pp. 581-82).

52 "The conservation [of substances] is a perpetual creation . . . and all change is a sort of transcreation" (Couturat, *Opuscules,* p. 635).

E is somehow extinguished and annihilated in [place] *B* and actually created anew and resuscitated in [place] *D*, which can be called, in new and most happy terminology, *transcreation*.[53]

This involves the continuous miracle which Leibniz later often deplores in criticizing occasionalism, but which he then regarded favorably, saying that "genuine and authentic miracles happen daily in nature." [54]

When his philosophy had matured Leibniz rejected transcreation, for by then he had a solution to the physical continuum problem which the doctrine of transcreation was constructed to evade. Writing to De Volder in 1699, Leibniz says:

I added the hypothesis of transcreation for the sake of illustration, speaking philosophically and particularly like the Cartesians, who say, with some ground, that God creates all things continuously. For them, therefore, moving a body is nothing but reproducing it in successively different places, and it would have to be shown that this reproduction cannot take place in leaps. Rather, this could not be shown without returning to the reason which I have proposed for the universal law of continuity. . . . However, this hypothesis of leaps cannot be refuted except by the principle of order, with the aid of the supreme reason, which does everything in the most perfect way.[55]

Let us now turn to Leibniz' mature theory of motion. In his *Dynamica* motion is defined as characterizing those bodies whose points do not remain in the same place, i.e., motion is temporal change of place.[56] Leibniz must hold motion to be a phenomenon, for this is the case with both space and time. Witness the following passage:

. . . matter and motion . . . are phenomena whose reality is rooted in the mutual perceptions of the things (at diverse times) and in the harmony with other perceptions.[57]

---

53 Couturat, *Opuscules,* p. 624; cf. p. 617.
54 *Ibid.,* p. 626.
55 *Phil.,* II, p. 193.
56 "That [body] is at rest whose every point remains in the same place. That [body] is in motion which does not rest" (*Math.,* VI, p. 320). One must note that the definition of *place* implies that this defines *relative* motion.
57 *Phil.,* II, p. 270. Cf. ". . . space, time, and motion each are in some degree an *ens rationis*" (*Math.,* VI, p. 247).

The phenomenality of motion is made necessary because, as we have pointed out, physical motion is *relative*.

> Motion, in mathematical rigor, is nothing other than the mutual change of position of bodies, nor is it anything somehow absolute, but consists in relation.[58]

This relational character of motion is alone sufficient, given Leibniz' intrinsic theory of relations, to relegate it to the realm of phenomena.

However, like all phenomena of the physical world, motion has its foundation in the monadic realm. For:

> . . . if there is nothing to motion than this mutual change [of place], it follows that nothing in nature affords a reason *(ratio)* for its being necessary to ascribe the motion to one thing [of those moving relatively] rather than to another. The consequence of this would be that there is no such thing as real motion.[59]

Thus motion can be studied from the starting point of its *fundamentum* in the real world. From this metaphysical point of view it must be absolute, not relative. When in his fourth letter Clarke urges that motion is a "really different state," and holds that this is negated by any theory holding physical motion to be relative,[60] Leibniz grants the former assertion, but questions the latter, saying:

> I reply that motion is independent of observation, but that it is not independent of observability.[61]

Leibniz holds that although motion in the physical world is indeed relative, it is absolute in the metaphysical world in virtue of its well founding, and so it is possible for God to tell which bodies are "really" in motion.[62]

> However, I agree that there is a difference between an absolute and genuine motion of a body and a motion simply relative to its position with respect to another body. For when the immediate cause of a change is in a body, it is genuinely in motion and then the position

---

58 Couturat, *Opuscules,* p. 590. Leibniz commends Descartes for having insisted on the relative nature of physical motion, but he reproaches him with having neglected this fact in his physics *(Phil.,* IV, p. 369; *Math.,* VI, p. 247).

59 *Phil.,* IV, p. 369.

60 *Phil.,* VII, p. 384.

61 *Ibid.,* p. 403.

62 This is possible for God alone, our observations giving no clues as to real motion. Hence, for us, an "aequivalentia Hypothesium" prevails here *(Math.,* VI, p. 247).

of the others with regard to it will change as a consequence, although the cause of this change does not reside at all in them.[63]

Thus, of a number of bodies in relative motion, only those are "really" in motion in which the *actual cause* of the change (*cause immédiate du changement* or *ratio mutationis*) resides.[64] Let us examine more closely the nature of this cause of motion.

As early as the dialogue *Pacidus Philalethi* (1676) Leibniz had maintained that whatever moves has a proper tendency to motion.[65] This constitutes an adumbration of the "solicitation to motion" with which we became acquainted in considering the ramified doctrine of force, a tendency to motion constituted by an infinitesimal *vis viva*.[66] Leibniz writes:

> . . . that which is real and absolute in motion consists not in what is purely mathematical, such as change in neighborhood or situation, but in motive force itself.[67]

Consequently the solicitation, like the *vis viva* itself, is derivative from the activity of monads, and so the *fundamentum* of motion is active primitive force. It is thanks to this well founding of motion that God, in virtue of his knowledge of the monadic world, is able to distinguish between true and merely relative motion.

Since no monad is without activity, it follows that no aggregate is wholly without *vis viva*. Consequently no body can be totally at rest:

> It is indeed true that, to speak exactly, there is no body whatever that is perfectly and entirely at rest, but, this is something from which one extracts in considering the matter mathematically.[68]

This accords beautifully with the principle of continuity. There is, in metaphysical strictness, no bifurcation of the bodies of the uni-

---

63 *Phil.*, VII, p. 404. To Arnauld, Leibniz writes, "movement of itself, *abstracting from its cause,* is always something relative" (*Phil.*, II, p. 57). Cf. the following proposed definition of motion: "that [body] moves [actually] in which there is present a movement of place [i.e., a relative motion] and moreover a cause (ratio) of motion" (*Math.*, VII, p. 20).

64 Again it must be remarked that Leibniz' use of the language of causal efficacy is metaphoric.

65 Couturat, *Opuscules,* p. 606. The reasoning is that the cause of motion must antedate movement.

66 See the remark later written by Leibniz on the ms. of the *Pacidus Philalethi* given in Couturat, *Opuscules,* p. 594.

67 Latta, *op. cit.,* p. 353.

68 *Phil.*, VII, p. 404.

verse into those at rest and those in motion. Such a division is a merely practical device.

Infinity

Not only was Leibniz concerned with continuity in philosophy and natural science, but as a mathematician he was eager to dispel the problems which arise in connection with it. The history of these problems goes back to the arguments of Zeno against motion and the many. The central issue can be put, How can a space or time-filling *interval* consist of points which do not fill space or instants which do not fill time? How can indivisibles constitute a continuum?

This problem Leibniz terms the *labyrinth* of the continuum and indivisibles.[69] Concerning it he writes:

> It is not possible to get a thread through the labyrinth concerning the composition of the continuum or concerning the greatest (maximum) and the least (minimum) and the unnamable and the infinite unless geometry gets it; in fact, no one arrives at a sound metaphysic except the man who comes over to it by that way.[70]

Leibniz did not dwell on the philosophic importance of this problem without having arrived at a solution to it that was satisfactory to himself. Before we can proceed to the study of this solution we must deal with *infinity*, another notion which is very important in Leibniz' thought.

Leibniz, on wholly logical grounds, rejects the notion of infinite number, holding that a definition must involve a proof of the possibility of the thing defined, as he had maintained earlier against Descartes' ontological proof.[71] It is this which invalidates the no-

---

69 See, e.g., *Phil.*, VI, p. 29.
70 *Math.*, VII, p. 326. Cf. the Platonic *mēdeis ageōmetētos eisitō*.
71 Thus in the *Meditationes de Cognitione, Veritate et Ideis* of 1684 Leibniz writes: "For we cannot safely (tuto) use definitions in deductions before we know that they are real definitions, i.e., that they involve no contradiction. The reason for this is that from notions which involve a contradiction one can simultaneously get opposite results, which are absurd. To make this point I like to use as an example the fastest motion, which implies an absurdity; we posit a wheel moving with the fastest motion—who doesn't follow me?—[and we also posit] an extended radius of the wheel which, at the end, moves faster than a nail in the circumference of the wheel, whose motion is therefore, contrary to the hypothesis, not the fastest" (*Phil.*, IV, p. 424).

tion of infinite number in Leibniz' view.[72] He did, however, attempt some qualitative approaches to the classification of infinites. For example, he distinguishes in the correspondence with Des Bosses between a categorematic infinity (which, he argues, cannot exist) and a syncategorematic and a supercategorematic infinity.

The denial of infinite number forces Leibniz to deal with two questions:

1. How, if infinitely large numbers are impossible, are the infinitesimals or infinitely small numbers demanded by the calculus possible?

2. How, if there is no infinite number, is an infinite variety of created things, or for that matter any of the infinities of the metaphysical world, possible?

The first question is on the whole consistently answered by a denial of infinitely small numbers. We find Leibniz writing to Bernouilli:

> For if we suppose that there actually exist the segments on the line that are to be designated by ½, ¼ . . . , and that all the members of this sequence actually exist, you conclude from this that an infinitely small member must also exist. In my opinion, however, the assumption implies nothing but the existence of any finite fraction of arbitrary smallness.[73]

In the light of later developments the corresponding argument against infinite number is pregnant: "For the greatest number is the same as the number (reading 'numero' for 'numerum'?) of all unities. However, the number of all unities is the same as the number (reading 'numero' for 'numerus') of all numbers. . . . Corresponding to any number you please there is given a companion number which is its double. Therefore the number of all numbers is not larger than the number of companion numbers; i.e., the whole is not greater than the part" (*Phil.*, I, p. 338; 1678).

The property that "the whole is not greater than the part" to which Leibniz objects in infinite collections came to be their defining characteristic. And if one uses the inequality $2^k > k$ instead of $2k \geqq k$ in Leibniz' argument against the number of all numbers, it becomes a well-known result of the modern theory of transfinite numbers.

[72] *Phil.*, I, p. 338.

[73] *Math.*, III, p. 536. Tr. by H. Weil, p. 44. Though Leibniz is not always so precise in his statements, he is quite consistent in his denial of infinitely small quantities. "If dx, d^2x, . . . , are, by a certain fiction imagined to remain, even when they become evanescent, as if there were infinitely small quantities . . ." (J. M. Child, p. 158). Leibniz' position is given in the assertion: "I consider infinitesimal quantities (to be) useful fictions" (*Phil.*, VI, p. 629).

The second problem resulting from the denial of infinite number, that of the infinite variety of the monads and their properties, is dealt with by maintaining that here there is a variety too rich to be encompassed by any numerical bound.[74] Such an infinity is the only one admitted by Leibniz; he terms it an *actual infinity*. It surpasses all numerical bounds in content, and is immeasurable by an infinite number.

This actual infinity is the darling of nature, which affects it everywhere.[75] The actual infiniteness of the real, as opposed to the finiteness encountered in the world of physics, is not the source of a gulf between physics and metaphysics. It is rather, Leibniz feels, the source of a wonderful agreement embodied in his philosophy. Thus he writes:

> It is found (turns out) that the rules of the finite succeed in the infinite, as if there were atoms . . . , and that vice versa the rules of the infinite succeed in the finite, as if there were infinitely small metaphysical [points].[76]

It is important for Leibniz to supply an answer to the question, How does an actual infinity avoid giving rise to infinite number, and thus lead to contradiction? The answer provides Leibniz with the saving thread for the continuum labyrinth. It proceeds from the remark that there are two ways of putting number to the variety of real things in the universe, and goes on to demonstrate that neither of these is legitimate.

1. One might regard the whole universe as one unity, and try to discern the constituents which make it up, thus counting its parts (a procedure which, of course, only God could undertake). But this cannot be done, for:

> The true infinity, strictly speaking, is only in the absolute, which exists before all composition and is not at all formed by the addition of parts.[77]

---

[74] In an essay of 1716, probably his last philosophical paper to have survived (see *Phil.*, VI, p. 487), Leibniz writes: "In spite of my Infinitesimal Calculus, I do not at all admit any true infinite number, though I concede that the multitude of things surpasses every finite number, or rather every number" (*Phil.*, VI, p. 629).

[75] "I am so much in favor of the actual infinite, that rather than admit that nature abhors it, as one says vulgarly, I hold that nature exemplifies it everywhere, in order to display better the perfections of her author" (*Phil.*, I, p. 416).

[76] *Math.*, IV, pp. 94-95.

[77] *Phil.*, III, p. 583.

The absolute whole can be divided, but not resolved into ultimate parts or constituents capable of enumeration, since there are certain kinds of wholes or unities which are logically prior to their parts, and therefore cannot be resolved into them. Leibniz gives the following example:

> Unity is divisible, but is not resolvable; for the fractions which are parts of unity have less simple notions, because integers (less simple than unity) always enter into the notions of fractions. Several people who have philosophized, in mathematics, about the point and unity, have become confused, for want of distinguishing between resolution into notions and division into parts. Parts are not always simpler than the whole, though they are always less than the whole.[78]

In accord with this argument, an actual whole, though divisible into actual parts, cannot be resolved into actual ultimate constituents, because the ultimate constituents are mere notions and have no reality.

2. There is the complementary way of assigning number to an infinite collection by a consecutive exhaustion of the individuals constituting that collection, but in the case under consideration this is not possible. The only reals are monads, and the collections to be numbered aggregates; these aggregates, being phenomenal, lack the unity requisite for enumeration. As Russell puts it, the position of Leibniz is that "one whole must be one substance, and to what is not one whole number cannot properly be applied." [79] Or, in Leibniz' own words,

> The "one" and the "existent" are [mutually] convertible, but as the "existent" is given through an aggregate, and so also is the "one," although the "existent" and the "one" are quasi-mental.[80]

But anything

> which is not one Being on its own account, but an aggregate, and has Arithmetical but not Metaphysical unity.[81]

In this way Leibniz excludes infinite number from the metaphysical world, and feels that he has achieved a reconciliation of infinite monadic plenitude with the paradoxes involved in infinite number.

We can now return to consideration of Leibniz' treatment of the

---

78 *Ibid.*
79 Russell, *Critical Exposition,* p. 116.
80 *Phil.,* II, p. 304. See the entire letter (to Des Bosses, 1706) (*Phil.,* II, pp. 304 ff.).
81 *Loc. cit.*

labyrinth of the continuum. It is by means similar to those employed in dealing with the infinite that Leibniz emerges from this labyrinth. We will proceed in two stages, first discussing the solution of the mathematical continuum paradox offered by Leibniz, and then how this solution is modified to eliminate the difficulties resulting from various instances of continuity in the metaphysical world.

Mathematical

Since the machinery used by Leibniz in the solution of this problem is exactly that employed in his treatment of the infinite, there is every reason to suppose that the historical development of the solutions went side by side.[82] Leibniz demanded that a sharp distinction be made between resolution into notions and division into parts, and between what is given as actual and what arises phenomenally. These distinctions he utilizes in his answer to the question of the relation of indivisibles and continuum.

Let us begin with the relation of point to line. Leibniz' position is perfectly explicit, though perhaps somewhat surprising: "A point may not be a constitutive part of a line." [83] This he explains by application of the remark that an infinite whole actually given does not have ultimately real components; these are mere fictions generated by an indefinite extension of a necessarily finite process.[84] Thus the line "is prior to its points since 'the whole is prior to the part, because the part is only possible and ideal'." [85] And so with

---

82 We chose to consider the problem of infinity first solely because of its logical priority. Note that the dichotomy of the ways of numbering—from ultimate constituents to whole, and from whole to ultimate constituents—parallels the dichotomy of the treatment of continuity into mathematical and metaphysical.

83 Wanke, *Das Steitigkeitsgesetz bei Leibniz* (Kiel: Die Universität, 1892), p. 9.

84 "And it is also in this way that mathematical points occur (come about), (for) they are also only modalities, that is to say extremities. And since everything is indefinite with respect to the abstract line, one here thinks in terms of all that is possible, such as the fractions of a number, without bothering about any actual divisions of the line" (*Phil.*, IV, p. 419). "And it is the confounding of the ideal with the actual that has completely confused everything, and which has generated the labyrinth [problem] of the 'composition of the continuum.' Those who compose (build up) the line with points have looked for first elements in ideal things, or for connections of a completely inappropriate kind" (*Phil.*, IV, p. 419).

85 *Phil.*, IV, p. 492.

the solution: "Points, to speak precisely, are extremities of extension, and not at all the parts constitutive of things." [86] Leibniz
emerges from the mathematical wing of the labyrinth of the continuum.

Metaphysical

The Leibnizian solution of the metaphysical continuum problem
is the complement to the mathematical solution. In the mathematical case difficulty was avoided because what was given as actual
or real, the mathematical continuum, could not be composed of
points which are mere ideal constructs. In the case of metaphysical
reals, i.e., the monads or metaphysical points, difficulty is avoided
because these cannot compose a real continuum. Any plurality of
monads has, as aggregate, a merely phenomenal reality, so that any
continuum they can compose is also merely phenomenal. Continuous quantities are thus to be assigned to the realm of phenomenal
possibility, not the realm of actualities, except insofar as the actualities involve a determination within possibilities.[87] Let me repro-
duce the argument in Leibniz' own words.

As was seen in the mathematical case, continuity occurs "where
the parts are indeterminate, and they can be taken in infinitely
many [alternative] ways." [88] Thus it follows that:

> A continuous quantity is something ideal which pertains to possibles
> and to actuals—in virtue of their being possibles as well. A continuum,
> that is, involves indeterminate parts, while, on the other hand, there
> is nothing indefinite in actual things, in which every division is made
> that can be made. Actual things are composed as a number is com-
> posed of unities, ideal things as a number is composed of fractions;
> the parts are actual in the real whole but not in the ideal whole.
> But we confuse ideal with real substances when we seek for actual
> parts in the order of possibles and indeterminate parts in the aggre-
> gate of actuals, and so entangle ourselves in the labyrinth of the con-
> tinuum and in inexplicable contradictions.[89]

Thus Leibniz holds that a continuum must have indefinite parts,
which is something that no collection of monads can have. For:

[86] Wanke, *loc. cit.;* cf. *Phil.,* III, p. 622.
[87] See the letter to De Volder of January 19, 1706.
[88] *Phil.,* IV, p. 392.
[89] *Phil.,* II, p. 282.

An indefinite is something like a continuum whose parts are not [given] in actuality, but can be taken [for consideration] arbitrarily, just like the parts of a unity, or fractions. If there were different subdivisions of organic bodies in nature, there would be different Monads. . . .[90]

The source of the difficulties which constitute the labyrinth of the continuum is failure to distinguish between the ideal or phenomenal and the real or actual. Leibniz grants that there would be trouble if both the indivisible constituent and the continuum to which it belongs could both at once be real, but this, he holds, cannot happen, and thus the collision between indivisible and continuum is prevented. In mathematics the continuum, the line, is real and the point is merely the ideal limit of an infinite subdivision. In metaphysics only the ultimate constituents, the monads, are actual, and any continuum to which they give rise is but phenomenal.[91] This is the Leibnizian solution of the paradoxes of the continuum.

A few words must be said as to the adequacy of this solution. One can, today, afford to be hard on Leibniz' treatment of the continuum problem. Subsequent developments in mathematics—the theory of transfinite numbers, point-set topology, measure theory— have shown that Leibniz' method of attack was poor. Indeed, Galileo had already handled the problem more satisfactorily, for Leibniz does not deal with the mathematical question of how indivisibles constitute a continuum, dismissing it with a remark that not both members of the associated pair, the continuum and its indivisibles, can be simultaneously or concurrently real. The meta-

---

[90] *Phil.*, II, p. 397.

[91] "With regard to those actualities in where only genuinely made divisions enter in, the whole is only a result or assemblage (of parts), like a flock of sheep; it is true that the number of simple substances which make up a conglomeration, however small, is infinite, since otherwise the soul which (causes) (makes) the real unity of the animal, the body of a sheep (for example), is genuinely subdivided, that is to say it is also a conglomeration of microscopic animals or plants, themselves composed (of parts) in addition to that which makes their real unity; and since this proceeds to infinity, it is clear that in the end, everything returns to these unities, the remainder or the results being nothing other than well-founded phenomena. . . . In actual, substantial things, the whole is a result or assemblage of simple substances, or in other words of a multitude of real unities. And it is the confusion of the ideal with the actual which has confounded everything and produced the labyrinth concerning the composition of the continuum" (*Phil.*, IV, pp. 491-92). Cf. *Phil.*, II, p. 268, and *Phil.*, III, p. 622.

physical problem is not solved satisfactorily either. He deals only with the case of continuity pertaining to aggregates, overlooking that it is also relevant when only monads are under consideration (e.g., in appetition).

With these brief critical remarks let us leave the exposition of Leibniz' views on infinity and continuity, and turn to an examination of the history of Leibniz' thought on these matters.

Before Leibniz one of the few fairly detailed discussions of infinity, infinite number, and continuity was in the *Discorsi* of Galileo.[92] Prior to Galileo the problem of how indivisibles can constitute a continuum had, from our point of view, been poorly treated. Galileo's solution was that points can make up a line provided there are enough of them. There are two types of infinity, an *intermediate* infinity (obtained by adding individual units one at a time without stopping), and a *true* infinity (*sibbene infinita*), far greater than the intermediate infinity. If one wishes to make up an extended continuum out of nonextended points, one must take a true infinity of them, for an intermediate infinity does not suffice.[93]

It is natural that Leibniz should have become interested in these questions during his stay in Paris when the calculus was born,[94] and turn to the works of Galileo for enlightenment. Understandably Leibniz felt dissatisfied with the somewhat bizarre infinite numbers of Galileo, and sought for a more satisfying view. But the *Discorsi* provided Leibniz with suggestions with which to develop his own view.

In the discussion of the first day Simplicio proposes the following "Peripatetic" solution to the mathematical continuum problem:

> My answer is that their number (i.e., the number of constituent points of a line segment) is both finite and infinite; potentially infinite but actually finite; i.e., potentially infinite before division and actually finite after division; because parts cannot be said to exist in

---

[92] I cite from the edition of the Northwestern U. Press, *Dialogues Concerning Two New Sciences*, 1946. The relevant material is given in the discussion on the first day.

[93] This solution anticipates, and on the whole for the proper reasons, that given in modern mathematics. To constitute a continuum, and be "space filling," a point set must be of cardinality C. Otherwise it cannot have positive Lebesgue measure (the condition on the cardinality is, however, not sufficient). If a point set has the (infinite) cardinality, i.e., is a Galilean intermediate infinity, its Lebesgue measure is O.

[94] 1672–1676.

a body which is not yet divided or, at least, marked out; and if that is not done we say that they exist potentially.[95]

This indeterminacy of parts is exactly what Leibniz regards as characteristic of the mathematical continuum. Galileo distinguishes between *division into parts* and *constitution by a true infinity of points,* doubtless the source of Leibniz' distinction between division into parts and resolution into notions.[96]

Proof of the Galilean source of Leibniz' treatment of the continuum problem is given by the constant reference to Galileo in Leibniz' first paper on mathematical continuity, the dialogue (in Galilean style) *Pacidus Philalethi* of 1676.[97] Here the essentials of Leibniz' solution of the mathematical problem, as we have already set it forth, are given, for this problem is discussed, and its solution summarized:

> For that reason it is not to be maintained that body or space is divided into points nor time into moments, because indivisibles are not parts but the extremities of [possible] parts; whence even if all things were subdivided, they would still not be entirely resolved into [ultimate] minima.[98]

Thus Leibniz' solution to the continuum problem, and his treatment of infinity, proceed by resorting to the distinction of actual and potential, and he reverts to the classical Aristotelian position combatted by Galileo. It must be noted that this solution accords admirably with Leibniz' philosophy, for it matches the division into real and phenomenal in such a way as to enable him to evade the continuum problem in his cosmology. The only price paid for this exit from the labyrinth is the reduction of the non-monadic to phenomenality, and this involves Leibniz in no additional commitments.

These considerations of Leibniz' views on infinity and continuity are an important component to a discussion of Leibniz' theories of space, time, and motion, for they enable him to evade the paradoxes of Zeno. Indeed they, together with the rule of well founding, supply the groundwork for these theories.

---

[95] Galileo, *Dialogues Concerning Two New Sciences,* p. 33.
[96] *Ibid.*
[97] Couturat, *Opuscules,* pp. 494-527. See also Gerhardt in *Math.,* VII, p. 809.
[98] Couturat, *Opuscules,* p. 623.

nine

MONADIC HIERARCHIES

The Union *versus* the Mere
Aggregation of Monads

We have already discussed Leibniz' teaching that monads can, and in general do, come together to form aggregates. The unity of such an aggregate is purely phenomenal: aggregates are not really individual *things;* they merely *appear* as such in the perceptions of (internal and external) observers. Leibniz' metaphysic does, however, have a place for composites whose unity is more than phenomenal. In his view, the natural realm does comprise real things whose unity is intrinsic and actual, rather than a mere matter of appearance to external observers.

Consider our everyday conception of a physical object. Why do we regard a drop of water, a grain of sand, or a tree as individual things, but not a cloud or a heap of sand or a stand of trees? Doubtless primarily because the former have a sort of "causal unity" the latter lack: when one part of a stone is turned, the other parts turn;

when part of a tree is burned, the remainder is affected; when part of a pebble is scratched, the vibrations are transmitted through the rest. The causal unity of a drop of water is relatively well-defined; when, for example, pressure is applied to one point, the others are deformed. A cloud, however, lacks such integrity; the particles of water that are its parts do not have a sufficiently close causal inter-relationship—its unity as *one individual thing* lies wholly in the eyes of the beholder.

This line of thought was espoused by Leibniz with respect to the unity of monadic aggregates, albeit with one important difference: the characteristically Leibnizian substitution of *perceptual* for *causal* unity. There are clearly two ways in which a collection of monads can become aggregated into a single and *unified* thing, either (merely) *externally* united in being perceived as one thing by an external observing monad (so that we have not a genuine union, but a union for someone), or *internally* and genuinely united by the mutual perceptions of the component monads. The former mode of unity is that of the water particles that make up a cloud; the latter is that of the grains of stone that make up a single rock. Moreover, there may in certain cases be not merely an extensive interlinkage of mutually clear perceptions, as with the monads making up a certain rock or plank of wood, but a highly structured network of clear reciprocal perceptions among the monads making up a complexly articulated organism, as a plant or animal. This latter case requires more extensive analysis, and will receive the attention it deserves in the next section, but a brief summary will be useful. When a monad perceives a *thing,* four major possibilities must be discriminated, in that the thing that is the object of perception may be: [1]

1. A simple *delusion* (e.g., a mirage).
2. A *disjointed aggregate* whose sole being as one thing is being perceived as such (e.g., a herd of animals, a cloud of water droplets).
3. A *unified aggregate* (e.g., a stick or stone).
4. A *structured aggregate* (e.g., a plant or animal).

---

[1] For Leibniz' own, more detailed scheme see the tabulation given in *Phil.,* II, p. 506.

Structured Aggregates of Monads:
Monadic Hierarchy

A unified aggregate, as we have characterized it, is an aggregation of monads whose reciprocal perceptions yield a pervasive and far-reaching degree of clear mutual perception and representation. Speaking in causal terminology, we would say there is a great deal of mutual interaction among the monads of such a group. It is possible, however, for an aggregate to attain to an even higher degree of unity when it is appropriately *structured*. What sort of structuring is at issue here?

Suppose that one monad of a collection perceives the others with a high degree of clarity, a circumstance that perdures through time so that the changes of state of the other monads are constantly represented with great clarity by the monad at issue. This monad is said by Leibniz to *dominate* the others and to be the *dominant monad* of the collection. Let it be assumed that such a situation is repeated over and over again somewhat as in the following diagram:

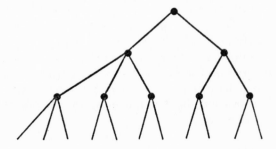

The topmost monad in the dominance hierarchy has access with reasonably high clarity to all or most of the perceptions of the subordinate monads. Here we have the groundwork for

> . . . the connection and order of things brings it about that the body of every animal and of every plant is comprised of other animals and of other plants, or of other living and organic beings; consequently there is subordination [of unit to unit], and one body, one substance, serves the other.[2]

---

2 *Théodicée,* §200.

The dominant monad is, so to speak, the central sensorium, for which the others stand in the role of subordinate organs. Because the respective states and changes of state of the whole system, the entire aggregate of monads, are pre-eminently presented in its dominant monad, this pivotal substance creates a unifying *substantial link* for the whole collection. Monadic dominance is, like everything else in Leibniz' world-system, a matter of monadic perception and agreement:

> . . . a dominant monad would detract [nothing] from the existence of other monads, since there is really no interaction (*commercium*) between them but merely an agreement (*consensus*). The unity of corporeal substance in a horse does not arise from any "refraction" of the monads but from a super added substantial chain [viz., the dominant monad] through which nothing else is changed in the (body-comprising) monads themselves.[3]

Since a single substance provides the focal unifying principle—what Leibniz (adapting an idea of Aristotle's) calls an *entelechy* [4]—we are entitled to consider such a hierarchically structured aggregate as a single individual, as opposed to a merely unified aggregate, such as the one whose "clear perception diagram" might be as follows:

The spirits (and souls) that are dominant monads being, like all monads, strictly independent, self-sufficient substances, why should they have need of a *body?* Of course they do not, strictly speaking, need it at all. Their inclusion in this best of possible worlds gives them a foothold in an orderly cosmos where everything is harmoniously accommodated to everything else within one

---

4 The term *entelechy* is sometimes applied by Leibniz to monads generally (e.g., *Monadology*, §56), but is usually restricted by him to monads capable of dominance, i.e., to souls and spirits.

all-embracing framework of ordering: "If spirits alone existed, they also would lack the requisite interrelation, and would be without the ordering of times and places."[5]

Souls and Spirits

When a group of monads is so organized that structured aggregate is iteratively piled upon structured aggregate, the highly ramified hierarchic structure that results gives rise to biological organisms. The sequence of cell:organ:plant (or animal) reflects this sort of structurization. When, as in animals (unlike plants), there is a highly centralized structure with one central monad dominating all the rest in its perceptions—even dominating the dominators of its organic constituents—we see exemplified the mode of monadic organization that typifies man and the higher animals.

In rough correspondence with the common-sense distinction, operative in the hierarchy

men
animals
plants
inert objects

Leibniz distinguishes among various sorts of unified aggregates with an increasing degree of hierarchical organization. In inert objects and at the lower end of the biological scale we find *bare monads,* but in plants and animals we have overriding dominance by a single all-predominant monad. In animals the dominant monad may be called a *soul* (*âme*) and is capable, by way of psychological capabilities, of sensation, consciousness, and memory. In man, and in the higher intelligences of whose existence in nature Leibniz feels assured, the dominant monad is a *spirit* (*esprit*), and is capable of reason, including the practical reason essential to moral agency. For Leibniz, the psychological capabilities and reason itself are functions that come into play at the higher levels of complexity in monadic organization.[6]

---

5 *Phil.,* VI, p. 172 (*Théodicée,* §120).
6 The angels (i.e., higher-than-human created rational beings) all have bodies (*Phil.,* II, p. 324). God alone is a pure, wholly incorporeal spirit (*Phil.,* VI, p. 546; cf. *Phil.,* V, p. 103; *New Essays,* Bk. II, Chap. i, §12).

Since they are monads, souls and spirits of course pre- and post-exist the bodies (monadic aggregates) they come to dominate:

> Those souls which one day will be human souls, like those of other species, have been in the seed, and in the progenitors as far back as Adam, and have thus existed always since the beginning of things, in some kind of organic body.[7]

They will ever continue in this best of possible worlds to play some role in the framework of organic nature.

Spirits are unlike the lower monads in that they mirror with relative clarity not only the monads of the created universe, but God as well. The spirits thus constitute the "City of God" that comprises, as we shall see, the locus of moral responsibility and moral goodness in nature.[8]

The difference between bare monads and spirits also manifests itself in the nature of appetition at these levels. One would not generally be justified in endowing monadic appetition with any status save that of the succession of perceptions—the onset of new perceptions and the termination of others. (Leibniz invites the analogy between monadic appetition and the first derivative of a mathematical function, indicating its rate of change at any particular point.) But, going beyond this in the case of spirits, Leibniz defines *will* as conscious appetition, and makes this metaphysical appetite the analogue to *conatus* in dynamics, i.e., to force. (In the early writings *conatus* is a minimal unit of motion, in the later a minimal unit of force.) Appetition at these higher levels points to the dimension of force in the metaphysical scheme.

Minute Perceptions

The dominant monad of a highly structured hierarchic aggregate, which Leibniz characterizes as the *entelechy* of the body represented by the aggregate, has all the monads of all its sub-aggre-

---

[7] *Phil.*, VI, p. 152; *Théodicée*, §91.
[8] PNG, §§84-89. It is a moot question for Leibniz whether a spirit ever fully loses its body (i.e., ceases to dominate some aggregate of monads) to the extent where it is incapable of functioning at at least a low level of consciousness. He answers the question in the negative. We shall pursue the matter in Chap. Twelve.

gates (organs) at its disposal with a more than ordinary degree of clarity.[9] Even when the dominance in question is a matter of a spirit's dominance over its body, these perceptions are neither *very* clear nor even conscious. Taken individually, as particular monad-of-monad perceptions, they are never conscious, and thus are never *actual perceptions* in our usual sense of the term. They are *minute perceptions (petites perceptions)* which—like the individual impacts of waves are lost as individual phenomena when we hear the pounding of the surf—are part of that aggregate phenomenon in which they collectively result. Every perception in our ordinary sense of the term is composed of infinite insensible perceptions.[10] Man's conscious perception is always *confused* perception. It is the aggregate effect of blending innumerable individual perceptions, each of which lies "beneath the threshold" (Leibniz has the concept but does not have this modern term) of noticeability.[11]

The theory of minute (unconscious) perceptions is, with Leibniz, an important part of psychological theory. Even spirits do not always enjoy full-bloodedly conscious perceptions, i.e., apperceptions. In sleep, for example, the dominant monad of a man's mind may or may not be conscious of certain perceptions, contrasting dreams with dreamless sleep. Although Leibniz maintains (with Descartes and against Locke) that a man's mind is always active, he holds (against Descartes) that the "thinking" in question is often altogether unconscious.[12] In the Cartesian view, the continuity of man's psychological life consists of the continuity of thinking, and thus of the unceasing performance of conscious acts. Leibniz, approving Locke's mockery of insistence upon the continuity of consciousness, finds psychic continuity in a shading of gradations of perceptions, apperceptions, sensation, and reflexive awareness that range over a wide area in clarity, vividness, and expressiveness, and lie, for the most part, below the horizon of conscious awareness. In holding this theory, Leibniz made a significant innovation in psychological theory to which we will return at greater length.

---

9 The expression "primitive entelechy" is, however, used by Leibniz to apply generically to *any* monad.

10 *Phil.*, V, pp. 105-7.

11 *Clear* perception in Leibniz is always a matter of monad-of-monad perception and, in the case of created monads, is (unlike *apperception = self-perception*) never conscious, save in the aggregate.

12 *Phil.*, V, p. 148.

The Vinculum Substantiale

There is but one way in which, in Leibniz' view, monadic aggregates can attain to a quasi-individuality, and become genuinely individuated things, "real unities." An aggregate can achieve this unity by virtue of the presence of a dominant monad (or *entelechy*), a monad of the system which, because of its hierarchic structuring, can perceive with a high degree of clarity all the other monads of the system, providing a sort of central receptor for their perceptions and, so to speak, using them as organs of perception and activity. Only the highest of the three grades of monads, spirits or minds, are capable of establishing a link which is sufficiently strong to give unity and individuality to the aggregate of monads containing it.[13]

Under such dominance the aggregate of monads attains to substantial form or substantial unity, the dominance situation providing the unifying linkage, the substantial bond (*vinculum substantiale*) which unites the aggregate into an individual.[14] A body without a dominant *entelechy* is merely a thing of aggregation, but with appropriate dominance it ceases to be a mere aggregate and becomes a true unity. The dominant monad creates a substantial bond among the intrinsically separate monads of the system, fusing them into a genuinely organic unit, and leading to a pluri-monadic entity that has authentic and intrinsic unity, not merely apparent unity for an external perceiver.

It should not be thought that an animal's, for example, dominant monad is the permanent proprietor of the aggregate of monads constituting his body.

> It is true, of course, that a soul cannot pass over from one organic body into another. . . . But it must be remembered that even this

---

[13] ". . . bodies are made only for spirits alone . . ." (*Phil.*, IV, p. 485). Leibniz is somewhat inconsistent here in limiting the type of monad capable of dominance to *spirits;* at most places it seems that both spirits and souls are able to dominate a system of monads—spirits for men, souls for animals.

[14] The justification of this representation of the matter is to be found in the correspondence with Arnauld (*passim*) in the *Système Nouveau,* and in the correspondence with Des Bosses (*passim*). See also A. Boehm's *Le "Vinculum Substantiale" chez Leibniz* (Paris: J. Vrin, 1938).

organic body remains *the same* in the way in which the ship of The-
seus or a river does; that is, it is in perpetual flux. And perhaps no
portion of matter can be designated which always remains the property of the same animal soul.[15]

Leibniz goes on in this connection to stress:

> This does not mean, as some who have misunderstood my thoughts
> have imagined, that each soul has a quantity or portion of matter ap-
> propriated to it or attached to it forever, and that it consequently
> owns other inferior beings destined to serve it always; because all
> bodies are in a state of perpetual flux, like rivers, and the parts are
> continually entering in or passing out.[16]

With respect to the organization of organic nature, Leibniz drew
upon each of the two rival genetic theories of his day: Malpighi's
theory of organic preformation and Harvey's theory of epigenesis.
According to the theory of preformation, the embryo of an organism is fully formed on a microscopic scale before incubation,
the subsequent incubation and development of the organism being
simply a matter of growth. In this theory, the entire biological development of an organism is not a matter of any genuine *origina-
tion,* but the continued unfolding of a pervasive organic pattern.
Opposing this view, the theory of epigenesis—principally derived
from microscopic study of the blood—views organisms as genuinely
originative from an organic material (the cells) endowed with the
capacity for growth, but lacking any predetermined impress of organic form. Leibniz seems to incline toward the theory of preformation at the level of the individual monad with its impressed organic
dynamism, and to adopt the standpoint of epigenesis regarding the
corporeal bodies of molar organisms.

Leibniz' correspondence with Father Des Bosses, who taught theology at the Jesuit school at Hildesheim, is of fundamental importance for an understanding of this aspect of his metaphysics.[17] It
is here that, in the course of a discussion of the dogma of trans-
substantiation, Leibniz develops in detail his concept of a *vinculum
substantiale,* a bond that can fuse into organized composite wholes
the "windowless" monads which are the ontological basis of his
metaphysical system. Leibniz' motives in espousing the views he

---

15 *Phil.,* II, p. 370 (Loemker, p. 970).
16 *Monadology,* §72.
17 This correspondence is given in *Phil.,* II.

presents in this correspondence with Des Bosses were called into question by Russell:

> In later letters, the doctrine [of the *vinculum substantiale*] is usually presupposed as the basis of discussion, and is employed to establish real matter and a real continuum. But nowhere does Leibniz himself assert that he believes it. He was extremely anxious to persuade Catholics that they might, without heresy, believe in his doctrine of monads. Thus the *vinculum substantiale* is rather the concession of a diplomatist than the creed of a philosopher.[18]

In view of this rebuke, classing the doctrine of a *vinculum substantiale* as a gratuitous feature of his philosophy introduced to accommodate Des Bosses, it is of interest to note that the contentions of Leibniz to which Russell objects are all to be found in Leibniz' correspondence regarding some points in the philosophy of physics with Burcher de Volder, a Cartesian who taught mathematics, physics, and philosophy at Leyden.[19] Though Leibniz does not here use the term *vinculum substantiale,* he presents all essentials of the doctrine in question. Moreover, Russell's doubt is quixotic on the very face of it: a man who explains to another at great length how the land lies need not make an issue of adding that that is how he believes it to lie. In short, it can be maintained with confidence that the positions at issue in Leibniz' conception of a *vinculum substantiale* were not "the concession of a diplomatist," but the exfoliation by a philosophical system-builder of an essential facet of his position.

---

18 Russell, *Critical Exposition,* p. 152.
19 Also given in *Phil.,* II.

ten

HUMAN KNOWLEDGE AND ITS CHARACTERISTICS

Truths of Fact and Truths of Reason

The dichotomy of truths into truths of fact (*vérités de fait*) and truths of reason (*vérités de raison*) is the cornerstone of Leibniz' theory of knowledge. Distinction between them can be drawn along three lines: 1) their source or "basis for being known" in the sense of *rationes cognoscendi;* 2) their mode of establishment upon their "grounds for being so" in the sense of *rationes essendi;* 3) their characteristic subject matter.

Truths of fact deal specifically with the *actual* world. We humans are wholly reliant upon experience for our acquaintance with them, for we can obtain knowledge of such truths only by perception (God alone can terminate the infinite analysis through which they can be established—but only with relative necessity—with respect to the Principle of Perfection). The grounds of the truths of fact hinge upon the will of God—they would be falsehoods rather than truths had He chosen it so. Truths of reason do not deal with matters of contingent existence but with generic truths that must hold good in every possible world.[1] (There is but one existential truth of this character, a noncontingent one, which asserts the existence of God.) Knowledge of such necessary truths is available, even to man, by conceptual analysis of a finitistic character. The status of these truths is independent of the will of God; they are as they are because the concepts involved in them are what they are.

As regards human (in contrast to divine) epistemology, there are then two distinct paths leading to two types of truth: perception (and apperception) leading, when employed properly, to truths of fact, and analytical reason leading, when correctly used, to truths of reason.

Perception and Apperception

Since we have dealt with perception thus far only in the generic way applicable unrestrictedly to all monads, special consideration must be given to some of its ramifications. Four modes of perception must be distinguished: 1) *ordinary monadic perception* as based on the mutual representation of all monads; 2) *minute* (i.e., unconscious) *perception* by the higher-grade monads of other monads; 3) the *confused perception* of monadic aggregates; 4) *apperception*, the reflexive self-perception of spirits. Monadic perception in its generic sense, based on the fact that the monads, though windowless, accord with one another in this best of possible worlds, applies throughout the monadic realm. The other modes, however, apply only to monads of the higher grades (viz., souls and spirits) and come into play only when these monads are the dominant monads of suitably complex aggregated organisms.

Minute perception and confused perception go hand in hand. When the dominant monad of a high-grade aggregate perceives confusedly the monads constituting some other aggregate, it perceives minutely some or most of the individual monads that constitute this aggregate. (Prosaically, when I, i.e., my dominant monad,

---

[1] Truths of fact, unlike truths of reason, thus have an essential existential component to the effect that the substances of this possible world are the ones that actually exist. The necessary, eternal truths, insofar as they deal with items of contingent existence at all, deal with them in a strictly hypothetical way (see *Phil.*, V, pp. 428-29). "Caesar crossed the Rubicon" typifies one case, "If Caesar crossed the Rubicon, then a man crossed a river" typifies the other.

see a chair, i.e., the monadic aggregate constituting the chair, then I in fact perceive confusedly the monads constituting the surface of the chair on my perspectival side—minutely perceiving them as individuals, but blurring these minute discrete perceptions into a confused whole.)

Apperception is the mode of perception distinctive of monads of the highest grade, the spirits. Leibniz succinctly defines apperception in the following terms:

> Thus it is well to distinguish between *perception,* which is the interior state of the monad representing outer things, and apperception, which is [self-] consciousness or the reflexive [or *reflective*] knowledge of this inner state.[2]

Apperception, then, is not consciousness as such (which is present in souls as well as spirits, in animals as well as man), but self-conciousness or self-perception generally, based on the capacity for reflexive self-revealing perception of the workings of one's own mind.[3] The procedure of some commentators in equating apperception with *conscious perception* in general [4] is not faithful to Leibniz' equation: apperception = *inner directed perception.* Leibniz' distinction between perception and apperception is in strict parallel to Locke's distinction between sensation and reflection, with consciousness in general present on both sides of the boundary, operative in regard to our awareness of both external things and internal states.

Innate Ideas

Since men cannot know the complete individual notions of contingent existents,[5] all human knowledge regarding truths of fact

---

2 PNG §4; *Phil.,* VI, p. 600.

3 Leibniz speaks of the *internal sense* "which may be called reflection; but this reflection is not limited to perceiving the mere operations of the mind, as is stated by Locke; it extends even to perceiving the mind itself . . ." (*Phil.,* V, p. 23). Cf. *Phil.,* V, pp. 107-8.

4 E.g., Latta, *op. cit.,* pp. 34, 121. There is some justification for this, since in §15 of the *Monadology,* Leibniz somewhat carelessly speaks simply of "apperception or consciousness." But of course *or* is sometimes used in the sense of *and* ("Doctors or lawyers may join").

5 ". . . it is not so easy to decide if the journey I intend to make is involved in my notion, otherwise it would be as easy for us to become prophets as to be geometers" (*Phil.,* II, p. 45).

must be based on perception and apperception. These are our only avenues of access to information concerning the contingently existing substances that populate the actual (best possible) world. If maintaining that only by observational experience can man obtain knowledge of "matters of fact and existence" makes the empiricist, then Leibniz is as much an empiricist as any.

Man's knowledge of particular facts about the realm of contingent existence is never *distinct* in the technical sense of this term which Leibniz adapted from Descartes:

> Knowledge is clear, therefore, rather than obscure when it makes it possible for me to recognize the thing represented. Clear knowledge, in turn, is either confused or distinct. It is *confused* when I cannot enumerate one by one the marks which are sufficient to distinguish the thing from others, even though the thing may in truth have such marks and constituents into which its concept can be resolved. Thus we know colors, odors, flavors, ... A distinct concept, however, is the kind of notion which assayers have of gold; one namely which enables them to distinguish gold from all other bodies by sufficient marks and observations.[6]

It is thus evident that man can never attain to better than confused (albeit clear) knowledge regarding contingent particulars, their nature (i.e., individual notions) being accessible to us only in piecemeal experience.

The case differs as regards the truths of reason, where we deal not with categorical truths about existing substance, but with 1) hypothetical truths about possible (or actual, the distinction is now indifferent) substances ("If Caesar is a general, and Caesar is in Rome, then a general is in Rome"), and 2) categorical truths about, not *substances,* but abstract *concepts* ("Primes greater than two are odd integers"). The first category reduces to the second, what is at issue being always a generic principle in which no essential reference to the specific substances is involved ("If anything is an X, and moreover is in place P, then an X is in place P").[7]

Such abstract truths do not hinge on perception: their truth does not depend upon any features of the actual world, nor do the items with which they deal, being abstract in character, (i.e., substances or aggregates thereof) with characteristics determined in experience. This line of thought leads us to Leibniz' doctrine of "innate ideas."

---

[6] Loemker, *Philosophical Papers and Letters,* p. 449.
[7] *Phil.,* V, p. 69.

Truths of the type "The sweet is not bitter" and "The red is not green" are analytic truths, truths of reason. This is due, from an epistemological angle, to their strictly hypothetical nature. *If* one recognizes, however obscurely, the concepts involved (sweet, red), which represent matters met with only in the realm of sense experience, *then* one needs no *further* experience to validate the truth at issue, but can do so solely by analysis of the now *ex hypothesi* known concepts.

In contrast with the truths of reason dealing with such sensory *concepts*—not, of course, sensory *facts*—there is a second, more important category of truths of reason which Leibniz calls innate truths (*vérités innées*).[8] These innate truths deal with innate ideas, that is, concepts which represent matters not met with only in the realm of sense experience. We may meet them, or rather approximations to them, within sensory experience, but they are idealizations constructed by the mind through reflexive probing into its own contents.[9] They deal not with the things of this world, but with those pertaining equally to every possible world. They are independent of perception, not in the sense that we may not learn of them in the course of experience, but that such experiences play a heuristic and not a determinative role. Leibniz' analogy is that experience helps us to such innate truths in the way in which miners come to expose a vein of ore, not by creating it as a result of their work as, for example, a painter, but by exposing a pre-existing material whose nature is wholly independent of their efforts and merely revealed by them. In holding that the concepts at issue in certain truths of reason are innate ideas, Leibniz does not mean to assert that infants are aware of them (that babies know about squares, circles, and numbers, for example). To be called innate, an idea or truth need not actually be known. Thus we find (in the *New Essays*) [10] this dialogue:

> L's Spokesman: . . . thoughts are acts, but the knowledge or truths known, being within us even when we do not think of them, are habitudes or dispositions. . . .

8 *Phil.*, V, pp. 68, 80.

9 The standard Leibnizian view is that the innate ideas cover the range of necessary truths, not only in logic and mathematics, but also in metaphysics. Thus, for example, in *New Essays*, Bk. II, Chap. i, §8, Leibniz' spokesman lists as innate ideas such "notions which the senses cannot give" as being, substance, unity, identity, cause, perception, and reason. Yet at an earlier stage of the discussion (Bk. I, Chap. i, §24) Leibniz had, clearly by way of a slip, confined the range to mathematics (in fact, arithmetic and geometry).

10 Bk. I, Chap. ii, §18.

Interlocutor: It is very difficult to conceive that a truth may be in the mind if the mind has never thought of that truth.

L's Spokesman: That is as if someone said it is difficult to conceive that there are veins in the marble before we have discovered them.

A Problem

Why did Leibniz not hold all ideas and all truths to be innate, as Russell contends he ought to have done?

> To the general theory that all truths which are known are innate, which Leibniz should have adopted, there is no answer but one which attacks the whole doctrine of monads.[11]

This criticism overlooks the important fact that Leibniz' conception of the innate is best construed in a quasi-spatial rather than a temporal sense. Granted that all that happens to any monad, all its perception and knowledge of truths of fact and truths of reason alike is eternally encapsulated within its defining complete individual notion. However, some of its perceptions are outward-oriented to other substances (what philosophers nowadays call *intentional*) and some are inward-oriented to itself (apperception). Certain ideas and truths are rendered innate, not by their failure to be built into a monad a priori, but by being wholly independent (logically rather than chronologically) of perceptions of the outward-oriented, intentional type.

Leibniz is thus able to draw the distinction between "innate" and "acquired" ideas and truths wholly *within* the ambit of his theory. His reconstruction of such a term as innate may be artificial, but this artificiality is at any rate perfectly harmless to the self-consistency and conceptual viability of his system.

Reason and the Universal Science

Leibniz distinguishes, with respect to the epistemology of human knowledge, among three faculties: sense, imagination, and reason.[12]

---

11 B. Russell, *Critical Exposition*, p. 163.
12 See especially the important epistle (to Queen Charlotte of Prussia) "On which is Independent of the Senses and of Matter" (*Phil.*, VI, pp. 491-508).

Sense deals with the sensory qualities encountered in the perception of external objects. The imagination, classed as an *internal sense,* adds to the individual senses the deliverances of the common sense, and thus introduces the "common sensibles" that provide the materials of mathematics. Reason brings us to the supersensible, i.e., the apperception of the mind's functioning even when not engaged in working with sensory materials. Here we encounter the materials for logic and metaphysics as well as the fundamental conceptions of ethics.

The materials of the truths of fact derive from sensation (i.e., conscious external perception); those of the pure truths of reason (innate truths) are inherent, and based, or at any rate basable, upon apperception. Knowledge of truths of reason is thus confined to spirits; souls (therefore the higher animals below man) are capable of sensation, consciousness *(attentio),* and memory,[13] but not of apperception, i.e., the *self-*consciousness requisite to apprehension of innate ideas. This fact is crucial for logical, mathematical, and metaphysical knowledge, as opposed to scientific knowledge. Leibniz frequently states that there are two empirical sources of data for knowledge, external and internal perception (reflection). The former gives the basis for scientific knowledge, but the latter alone supplies the materials for metaphysics, since it is the source of our knowledge of such categories as substance and causality, and also provides the foundation of the "personal identity" needed for moral responsibility, as distinguished from metaphysical or monadic identity. (To experience the latter would require a knowledge of the law of one's individual nature.)

Reason has two basic capacities with respect to its materials, the ideas: *analysis,* by which these ideas are dissected into their component ideas, and *comparison,* by which the coincidences and differences between the components of two ideas can be noted. The fundamental resources of human reasoning are extremely simple, but their systematic, component application leads to the endless complexities of our knowledge.

Notwithstanding his classification as a rationalist, Leibniz does not think that any empirical science can be deduced from metaphysical first principles. He does think of the empirical facts as "grounded in" metaphysical truths (via the Principle of Sufficient

---

13 *Phil.,* VII, p. 529; *Phil.,* VI, p. 610.

Reason),[14] but deduction is no more at issue here than Kant believed that Newtonian astronomy can be deduced from the Principle of Causality. The principles in each case provide only the general framework for a generic *mode* of justification. Leibniz leaves no room for doubt that on the side of *human* epistemology, he is a strict empiricist; the detailed content of an empirical science must be obtained through experiment by *observation*.

Always important in his thinking was Leibniz' program of a universal science (*scientia universalis*) for coordinating all human knowledge, providing an architectonic framework within which each of the particular sciences, while functioning efficiently in its own area, would stand in illuminating relation to the rest. This program comprised two parts: 1) a universal character or notation (*characteristica universalis*) by use of which any item of information can be recorded in a natural, simple, and systematic way, and 2) a formalized method or calculus for reasoning (*calculus ratiocinator*), manipulating the knowledge recorded in a computational fashion to reveal the logical consequences of any item and its interrelation with others. The project of a universal character was to serve several functions: provide a simplified notation for science, a medium of international communication, and a ready source of information to facilitate scientific discovery and demonstration. It was by no means original with Leibniz, but was, as one recent scholar puts it, "an intellectual commonplace in seventeenth century Western Europe." [15] The conception of a calculus ratiocinator, however, was original with Leibniz, and led him to develop mathematically inspired systems for reasoning in a way that makes him the unquestioned founder of modern symbolic logic.[16]

In his early *Dissertation on the Art of Combinations* [17] Leibniz sought to take steps toward developing "science of the sciences" along mathematico-logical lines. He worked in terms of his subsequently standard approach of beginning with basic general concepts and, by their combination, building up complexes which can

---

[14] It is just this he has in mind when he writes to Arnauld, in a most misleading formulation, that "I reduce all mechanics to a single metaphysical principle" (*Phil.*, II, p. 62).

[15] L. J. Cohen, "On the Project of a Universal Character," *Mind*, vol. 63 (1954), pp. 49-63.

[16] See L. Couturat, *La logique de Leibniz* (Paris: Felix Alcan, 1901).

[17] *Phil.*, IV, pp. 27-102. This work, written in 1665 and published in the following year, was Leibniz' first substantial philosophical essay.

then be analyzed into their basic constituents. This combinatorial procedure underwrites the possibility of substituting mathematical computation for conceptual analysis, for "characters can be applied to ratiocination [because] there is in them a kind of complex mutual placing (*situs*) or order which fits the things [represented], if not in the single words at least in their combination and connection." [18]

For the purposes of a somewhat crude illustration, consider the correspondence of concepts to index-numbers:

2–dog
6–spaniel
7–male
11–female

A *female spaniel* would get the index-number $66 = 6 \times 11$. The fact that this includes 2, the index-number for *dogs,* among its divisors underwrites the truth of the proposition that *Every female spaniel is a dog.* With this approach we could also guarantee through computation the validity of such a syllogistic inference as

All M is P
All S is M
All S is P

since when we know that $\#(P)$, the index-number for $P,$ is a divisor of $\#(M)$, and that $\#(M)$ is a divisor of $\#(S)$, $\#(P)$ must also be a divisor of $\#(S)$. Development of complex arithmetical schemes for the accommodation of logical inferences was a lifelong preoccupation which Leibniz carried to a high degree of sophistication and adequacy.

Error

In regard to truths of reason, error can come about only through heedlessness or carelessness—that is, through an outright mistake. This can occur 1) in the analysis of a concept by an oversight or omission of something that belongs to it or by the careless or inadvertent insertion of something that does not, or 2) in the comparison of two concepts, either in erroneously finding a feature in

---

[18] *Phil.,* VII, p. 192.

one concept in which it is not really present, or in failure to note that a feature actually present in one is also present in the other. Errors concerning truths of reason thus come about essentially either through mistakes in calculation (due to lack of attention) or in memory:

> There can be no doubt in mathematical demonstrations except insofar as we need to guard against error in our arithmetical calculations. For this there is no remedy except to re-examine the calculation frequently or to have it tested by others so as to add confirmatory proofs. This weakness of the human mind arises from a lack of attention and memory and cannot be completely overcome, and Descartes' allusion to it, as if he knew of a remedy, is in vain.[19]

The mention of lack of attention points to carelessness as a prime source of error in this sphere, and mention of memory points to Leibniz' Platonic doctrine that the truths of reason lie buried in the unconscious recesses of man's memory.

Error in regard to truths of fact comes about through illusion or delusion. Either 1) we may mistake what we sense, imputing to some actual external aggregate of monads, on inadequate or misinterpreted sensory evidence, a feature which does not reflect the actual condition of the aggregate (as, for example, in a case of mistaken identity; this possibility is built into the confused nature of perception); 2) we may, in the case of outright delusion, simply impute to the external world of monads aggregational features for which there is no adequate basis (e.g., a mirage), that is, which have no appropriate basis external to the misperceiving monad. This second is never, as with Descartes, a matter of sheer willfulness without any adequate basis whatsoever, but always has *some* foundation, however tenuous, in the sphere of monadic realities.

The Unconscious

Leibniz' doctrine of unconscious perception (*petite perception*) may be seen as a bold stroke of innovative genius in the history of psychology, but it may also be seen in the less dazzling light of an inescapable necessity of Leibniz' system. Consider two of Leibniz' commitments: 1) every monad always perceives (the contempo-

---

[19] *Phil.*, IV, p. 356.

raneous state of) every other monad with a greater or lesser degree of clarity; 2) the human mind is a monad—the dominant monad of the highly structured aggregate that is the human body. Given these two commitments, the concept of unconscious perception is, for all practical purposes, an unavoidable result. They demand a theory that admits of perceptions below the threshold of conscious awareness.

As opposed to Locke, Leibniz maintains the Cartesian teaching that the spirit always thinks. This thought, however, need not be conscious. A spirit (like any monad) will never be without perceptions, but will often be without *apperceptions* (conscious perceptions), whenever, for example, we have no distinct perceptions, as in deep sleep.[20] The unconscious as it relates to petites perceptions in Leibniz' theory of psychology is not, of course, to be thought of along Freudian lines. Rather, it can be viewed in light of the Fechner-Weber approach in explaining conscious molar experiences by reference to their origin in micro-events serving as their stimuli at the physiological level.

The higher-grade monads (souls and spirits) are capable of memory, i.e., perceiving stages of their own past. Traces of all that happens to such monads at one juncture are found at all later junctures. But the monads are not always consciously aware of their entire past; the retrospective perceptions are for the most part very weak, and entirely unconscious. Nevertheless, the petites perceptions play a very important role in providing for the continuity of psychic life: [21]

> These insensible perceptions also identify and constitute the same individual who is characterized by the traces or expressions which they preserve of the preceding states of this individual, in connecting them with his present state. . . . But they (namely these perceptions) even provide the means for recovering this recollection. . . . It is for this reason that death can only be a sleep and cannot indeed continue, the perceptions merely ceasing to be sufficiently distinguished, and reduced in animals to a state of confusion which suspends consciousness, but which cannot last always; not to speak here of man who must in this regard have great privileges in order to preserve his personality.[22]

---

[20] *Phil.*, V, p. 148; *New Essays*, Bk. II, Chap. xix, §4.
[21] We return here to the Leibnizian leitmotiv of continuity, already touched upon in Chap. Four.
[22] *Phil.*, V, p. 48.

Leibniz specifically likens man's physiological state of "losing consciousness" in periods of fainting or dreamless sleep, during which we have no distinct apperception and of which we later remember nothing, with the ordinary perceptions of the bare monads from which this "does not sensibly differ." [23]

Not only can a man's mind (*spirit; esprit*) have unconscious perceptions—a feature it shares with the soul (*âme*) of an animal—but it can also have unconscious apperceptions. This is somewhat surprising; it might seem that when we are self-conscious (i.e., aware of being aware of something) we must *ipso facto* be aware of this awareness. But against this view Leibniz redeploys the infinite regress argument, already found in Aristotle,[24] to the effect that:

> it is impossible for us always to reflect explicitly upon, i.e., be reflexively aware of, all of our thoughts; otherwise the mind would make a reflexion upon each reflexion *ad infinitum* without ever being able to pass on to a new thought.[25]

The iterative piling-up of reflective awareness of reflective awareness must stop somewhere, and the conception of unconscious apperception provides a convenient means of termination.

As these explanations indicate, Leibniz does not give the unconscious a prominent place in his account of the psychology of spirits on grounds of any specifically empirical investigation of actual features of human perception and thought. He was compelled to the development of his theory of the unconscious by the systematic exigencies of his view of the mind as a monad.

Memory

Memory, for Leibniz, comes near to being a cross between perception and apperception. In perception a (i.e., any) monad represents the states of other monads; in apperception a (highest-grade) monad reflects the contemporary state of itself; with memory the higher-grade monads (souls and spirits) reflect states of their own past.

---

23 *Monadology*, §20.
24 *De anima*, 407a10 ff.
25 *Phil.*, V, p. 108.

Memory is the key to the individuation through time of the spirits (monads; *esprits*), i.e., their continuing self-identity *as spirits*. As a monad, every spirit has a definitive, complete, historically continuous self-identity built into its characterizing program, but this would not guarantee its permanence and continuing self-identity as a spirit, rather than merely as a substance. When in the course of its history a monad once attains to the status of a spirit, coming to dominate a suitably complex aggregate of monads, it retains this status forever (for reasons to be explored in Chapter Twelve, but ultimately vouched for only by the fact that this is the best of possible worlds). It will always retain some suitable retinue of monads to dominate, perhaps dropping for a time to the status of a lower-grade soul, but never losing its status as a better than bare (inorganic) monad, and never losing its capacity for dominance of high-level complex aggregates. Moreover, a spirit never wholly loses the memory of its conscious experiences, although this memory may itself lapse into unconsciousness for stretches of time. A spirit will always look forward to future periods of high-level activity.

Leibniz' teaching of the permanently elect status of spirits is partly a matter of theological accommodation. It is not a theorem, but a side-product of the system; it is certainly not an inevitable (or even plausible) consequence of the fundamental theses of his metaphysical system.

eleven

LEIBNIZ' ETHICS

The Good Life

The Lockean spokesman in the *New Essays* (Philaretes) is made to voice the ancient view that moral principles are not natural (*physei,* by nature), but man-made (*thesei,* by convention):

> Moral good and moral evil is the conformity or the opposition which is found between voluntary acts and a certain law which brings us (physical) good and evil by the will and power of the lawgiver. . . .[1]

This "will of the lawgiver" is not, as with Hobbes, an essentially arbitrary matter. A right will, specifically including even God's will, is subject to objective and nonarbitrary moral standards.[2] It is against this background that Leibniz' spokesman (Theophilus) develops his position:

> The previous view not being the ordinary sense that is given to morally good and virtuous acts, I prefer for myself, to take as the

---

[1] *New Essays,* Bk. II, Chap. xxviii, §5; tr. A. G. Langley.
[2] See the important essay, *Reflections on the Common Concept of Justice* in *Philosophical Papers and Letters,* ed. L. E. Loemker (Chicago: University of Chicago Press, 1956), pp. 911-32, where the relevant issues are canvassed in substantial detail.

measure of moral good and of virtue the invariable rule of reason which God is charged with maintaining.[3]

The good life (the moral life) being that lived in accordance with "the invariable rule of reason," the principles of action and justice are codified in two sorts of laws: the divine law (natural and positive) and the civil law (always positive). The social relativity—variability from group to group—of all positive law is recognized, but discounted on the grounds that mistakes are here, as elsewhere, possible:

> Although you [Philaretes] admit that men claim to speak of that which is naturally virtuous or vicious according to immutable laws, you maintain that in fact they mean to speak only of that which depends on opinion. But it seems to me that by the same reasoning you could further maintain that truth and reason and all that could be named as most real, depends on your opinion, because men are mistaken when they judge of it. Is it not better then on all accounts to say, that men understand by virtue as by truth, that which is conformed to nature, but that they are often mistaken in its application; and besides they are mistaken less than they think.[4]

This conception of morality as *action in consonance with general principles of conduct that are conformed to nature* endows Leibniz' ethics with a rigidly legalistic cast that reflects not only his legal training, but also his mathematician's penchant for an orderly system of general principles, and his susceptibility to the influences of Catholic theology.

"Evil," writes Leibniz, "may be taken metaphysically, physically, and morally. Metaphysical evil consists in simple imperfection, physical evil in suffering, and moral evil in sin." [5] Physical and moral evil go back to, and are forms of, metaphysical evil; at present only moral evil, i.e., *sin,* concerns us here. What, according to Leibniz, is its nature? The answer is forthcoming within the legalistic framework of Leibniz' ethics: *transgression,* violation of "the law," especially knowing and calculated transgression. The root source of morals and politics is the disinterested love of others, based on recognition of their intrinsic merit. This, according to Leibniz, generates *natural right* in its three degrees: *"strict right (jus strictus)* in commutative justice, *equity—*i.e., *charity* in the

3 *New Essays,* Bk. II, Chap. xxviii, §5.
4 *Ibid.,* §10.
5 *Phil.,* VI, p. 115.

narrower sense—in distributive justice and *piety* (or probity) in universal justice." [6] These varieties of justice define the precincts of law, both positive and moral, and highlight the intimate linkage between them.

Obedience to the law is easier and more certain when we know exactly what the law states—what it in fact requires. This brings up the question of the nature and source of the rules of right action which codify the principles of conduct that are definitive of the good life.

The City of God

Only the highest class of monads, the spirits, fall within the purview of ethical considerations. They alone are capable of self-consciousness (*apperception*), and thus they alone can perceive the moral coloration of their own actions as right or wrong. As the sole created existent capable of conscious choice and intelligent action, a spirit "imitates, in its own province and in the little world in which it is allowed to act, what God does in the great World." [7] Human life in its ethical, cultural, and aesthetic perspective is a separate dimension of the physical and organic realm. It is a "moral world within the natural world." [8] Forming the population of the City of God, over which God is monarch, the spirits owe each other that mutuality of common concern that reflects in miniature God's prime concern for the welfare of the spirits in his creative choice of the best possible universe. The goal of Leibniz' social philosophy is the creation of a universal society which mirrors the great Kingdom of spirits, of which God is the head. (This ethical motive seems to be one of the main reasons for Leibniz' insistence upon the omnitemporality of spirits, i.e., the fact of their co-eternality with the world.) [9] The work of ethical theory thus flows into the metaphysic of the monadic hierarchy: in action, as in knowledge, God provides the ultimate, infinitely removed, ideal. This ideal is one

---

[6] *Phil.*, III, p. 386. From the "Preface to the *Codex Juris Gentium Diplomaticus*" (1693).
[7] PNG, §14.
[8] *Monadology*, §86.
[9] Cf. *Phil.*, VI, p. 517.

which the moral man should, and the family of spirits on the whole does, hold constantly before himself; the free activity of the spirits is aimed at and works toward it. Here we have Leibniz' vision of the great purposive scheme of creation—universal progress toward perfection, directed toward a *telos* that is ever goal but never destination; movement without arrival, improvement without perfection.

In good action the example of God, the will of God, and the welfare of one's fellows come together in an indissoluble unity. Leibniz writes:

> The good is that which by the general institution of God is conformed to [i.e., rendered conformable by] nature or reason.[10]

Since God's goodness is embodied in nature, his creation, we can learn the principles of ethics—the canons of human welfare—from scientific study of the rational structure of this *modus operandi* in this sphere. The scientific study of nature not only points the way toward the good life, but also puts into our hands the tools by which the prime aim of ethics, the advancement of human welfare, can be achieved. In his projects for advancing the sciences and his promotion of learned academies and institutions, Leibniz sought to implement his own ethical commitments according to his best abilities. For him, reunion of the churches, for example, was a preeminently feasible and *moral* goal: since truth is one, and human spirits are citizens of the City of God, one theological system should be able to unite the religious principles of all right-thinking men. (Think here of Nicholas of Cusa's motto of *una religio in rituum varietate*.)

An Apparent Discrepancy

Leibniz' fondness for the City of God conception, with its corresponding emphasis upon the welfare of the spirits, betrays him into one of the few discrepancies of his system. He is, as we saw above,[11] fundamentally committed to the criterion of a "best pos-

---

10 *New Essays*, Bk. II, Chap. xxviii, §5.
11 In Chap. One.

sible" world as one that exhibits "the simplest laws with the richest phenomena." This highly metaphysical conception of goodness seems in a possible relationship of tension with a more emphatically moral criterion acknowledging God: primary responsibility to the spirits.[12] In one important discussion, however, he makes it clear that he is prepared to see the metaphysical considerations prevail over the ethical ones, in the final analysis:

> If there is more evil than good in intelligent creatures, there is more evil than good in all God's work. . . . I do not admit it because *this supposed inference from the part to the whole, from intelligent creatures to all creatures, assumes tacitly and without proof that creatures devoid of reason cannot be compared or taken into account with those that have reason.* But why might not the surplus of good in the non-intelligent creatures that fill the world compensate for and even exceed incomparably the surplus of evil in rational creatures? It is true that the value of the latter is greater; but by way of compensation the others are incomparably greater in number; and it may be that the proportion of number and quantity surpasses that of value and quality.[13]

Universal Justice and True Wisdom

In Leibniz' ethical fragments,[14] which largely occupy themselves with clarification of the key concepts, a trilogy of definitions recurs time and again: [15]

> *Wisdom* is the science of happiness.
> *Virtue* is the habit of acting in accord with wisdom.
> *Justice* is the charity of the wise man, i.e., that which is congruent with the will of the good and prudent man.

The basic convention here is that of human happiness (félicité, bonheur, *felicitas*) defined as "a durable state of pleasure" ("un

---

12 This tension comes out clearly in the important passage in *Phil.*, IV, p. 462. The idea that this tension is resolvable, and indeed resolved, in this "best possible" world is a fundamental act of faith with Leibniz (see *Phil.*, VI, p. 605; PNG, §15).

13 *Phil.*, VI, pp. 377-78. Our italics.

14 For these see primarily Gaston Grua, *G. W. Leibniz: Textes inédits*, 2 vols. (Paris: Presses Universitaires de France, 1948).

15 *Ibid.*, Vol. II, pp. 579 ff.

Estat durable de plaisir," *status laetitiae duraturae*).[16] Pleasure is the starting-point, for:

> . . . the impulse to action arises from a striving toward perfection, the sense of which is pleasure, and there is no action or will on any other basis. Even in our evil purposes we are moved by a certain perceived appearance of good or perfection, even though we miss the mark, or rather pay for a lesser good, ill sought, by throwing away a greater. Nor can anyone renounce (except merely verbally) being impelled by his own good, without renouncing his own nature.[17]

Wisdom is called upon the scene because morally relevant action is always guided by thought; man acts as he *sees fit* to act. Errors of action derive from errors of understanding, much as with Descartes. There are, basically, two sorts of human freedom: freedom of the will *to do what seems best,* and freedom of the understanding to pursue its inquiries *to get clear* on the issues. The will should not be permitted to stray beyond the limits of proper understanding, and lead us into action before the understanding has thoroughly canvassed the relevant considerations:

> It is therefore incumbent on the soul to be on its guard against misleading appearances, and by a firm resolve to reflect and only to act or judge in certain circumstances after mature deliberation.[18]

Haste and heedless enthusiasm must be avoided at all costs. The maxim *Pas trop de zèle* could have originated with Leibniz. Wisdom teaches us the proper course of its pursuit; virtue is the habit of acting wisely; justice is the "charity" of the wise man who puts the happiness of others on a par with his own: the good and just man chooses his actions to conform with the general good.[19] There should be no divergence here, because ". . . the happiness of those whose happiness pleases us is obviously built into our own, since things which please us are desired for their own sake." [20]

It thus transpires that:

> There is a twofold reason for desiring the good of others: one *is* for our own good, the other *as if* for our own good. . . . But, you ask, how is it possible that the good of others should be the same as our

---

16 *Ibid.,* p. 613.
17 *Phil.,* III, p. 389.
18 *Phil.,* IV, p. 454; *Discourse on Metaphysics,* §30.
19 Note the axiom "Whatever is of public utility is to be done" (*Quicquid publice utile est, faciendum est*). *Phil.,* IV, p. 613.
20 *Phil.,* III, p. 386.

own and yet be sought for its own sake? For otherwise the good of others can be our own good only as a means, not as an end. I reply on the contrary that it is also an end, something sought for its own sake, since it is pleasant.[21]

The good act is that which makes for the public good; ethics and politics coalesce.[22] Leibniz' ethic is of a strictly proto-utilitarian character, and is, despite its apparently theocentric origins, wholly secular in orientation. To be sure, the good man must "do God's will," but since this will places prime value upon the well-being of that community of spirits whose head is God Himself, it is inevitably God's will that man should act for the benefit of his fellows. For Leibniz, all ethically sound human action is oriented toward working out the great design of creation—realization of God's kingdom in this world. The unity of God's plan and of the ethical scheme is one of the constitutive harmonies definitive of the best possible world.

Leibniz harks back to the Greeks, and anticipates the utilitarians, in the pivotal role his ethical theory accords to *knowledge*. Moral goodness is not a matter of faith, inspiration, or good will, but of *right action*, defined as action that makes for the benefit of the human community. But this is patently a matter of knowledge. The person who can best help an injured man is not just the man of good will but the trained physician, so the person who can best act for the interest of his fellow men is he whose knowledge of the nature of man and of his natural environment can effectively guide his deliberations for action. The pursuit of knowledge itself becomes a major imperative in ethics; wisdom and goodness are joined by an unbreakable bond:

> There are people today who consider it clever to declaim against reason. . . . [But] if those who mock at reason spoke in earnest, it would be a new kind of extravagance unknown to past centuries. To speak against reason . . . is to speak against one's self, against one's own good, since the principal point of reason consists in knowing the truth and following the good.[23]

In his emphatic stress on reason, Leibniz is a child of his century and a colleague of Spinoza, as in the strikingly Spinozistic passage:

> . . . since the power peculiar to the mind is understanding, it follows

---

21 Loemker (ed.), *Philosophical Papers*, p. 213.
22 See the opuscule entitled *Politica ab ipsa Ethica non est distincta. Ibid.*, p. 563.
23 *New Essays*, Bk. II, Chap. xxi, §50.

that we will be the happier the clearer our comprehension of things and the more we act in accordance with our proper nature, namely reason. Only to the extent that our reasonings are correct are we free and exempt from the passions which are impressed upon us by surrounding bodies.[24]

Moral Reasoning and Moral "Instinct"

Ethics, according to Leibniz, cannot be framed in the strict pattern of a demonstrative science because there are no self-evident (i.e., analytically true) truths of reason that could serve as its axiomatic first principles.

> And, although you can truly say that ethics has principles which are not demonstrable, and that one of the first and most practical is, that we ought to pursue joy and avoid sorrow, it is needful to add that this is not a truth which is known purely by reason, since it is based upon internal experience. . . .[25]

Certain rules of morality are, however, fundamental, including preeminently these two:

1. The egocentric hedonic principle that man "ought to pursue joy and avoid sorrow."
2. The social principle of the golden rule which is the foundation of all rules of justice: *Do to another only what you would have him do to yourself.*

Knowledge of these rules is arrived at by insight, and their acceptance is underwritten by instinct. These basic moral rules are innate in that they are not based on external experience, but are an internal drawing on the resources of our own minds. By applying the basic rules, other subordinate rules can be derived by strict reasoning, and thus a (deductive) science of morality is possible. Practical reasoning in situations involving choice (volition) can be carried on by the application of the system of practical principles. Most men, however, do not act on the basis of moral reasoning, but by instinct:

> As morality . . . is more important than arithmetic, God has given to man *instincts* which prompt at once and without reasoning to some portion of that which reason ordains; just as we walk in obedi-

---

24 Loemker (ed.), *Philosophical Papers,* p. 431.
25 *New Essays,* Bk. I, Chap. ii, §1.

ence to the laws of mechanics without thinking of these laws. . . . But these instincts do not prompt to action in an invincible way; the passions may resist them, prejudices may obscure them, and contrary customs alter them. Nevertheless, we agree most frequently with these instincts of conscience, and we follow them also when stronger impressions do not overcome them.[26]

What for the truly wise man is knowable through "moral science" —intuitive insight into basic principles and subordinate maxims derivable by practical reasonings therefrom—is by the grace of God made immediately accessible through instinct. Despite emphasis on reason, this recourse to instinct makes ample room for unthinking goodness and *fides rustica*. In Leibniz' view the highest forms of virtue are perhaps the private preserve of the highest human intellects, but the elemental requisites for the good life lie within the reach of all.

The greatest felicity within man, however, is to enter under the guidance of reason into the profound truths of mystical theology, thus to sense and respond to the Love of God. This love, the highest possible attainment of the human soul, is a sure consequence of the progress of true knowledge of nature and metaphysics.[27] Man's reason is his main road to true happiness, thus man's natural instinct to seek pleasure and avoid pain will lead him, following the direction of reason, to the highest happiness he can attain. This is why "Wisdom is nothing but the science of happiness itself." [28]

Man's Action and God's Perfection

Critics of Leibniz have long fixed on two questions as loci of special difficulty for him. Given that God's creation—choice of a particular spirit—is made in terms of its complete individual notion that includes every detail of its entire history: 1) How can we speak of "voluntary action" or "free will" at all? 2) How can we impute moral coloration (as praiseworthy or blameworthy, right or wrong) to a substance whose very existence, and consequently capacity to act, is a matter the responsibility for which rests, not with that substance itself, but with God?

---

26 *Ibid.,* §9.
27 Grua (ed.), *Textes inédits,* Vol. II, p. 23.
28 *Phil.,* III, p. 386.

The first question is more easily dealt with, for voluntary action is a mode of action, and the general strategy by which Leibniz finds a place for activity within his strictly deterministic scheme can be made to do the necessary work here. A substance acts, according to Leibniz, when it initiates a change of subsequent modifications. It acts "freely" when the substance at issue is a spirit. Its action is the result [29] of inner spontaneity, of a course of rational deliberation as to the eligibility of alternatives, i.e., a deliberate choice among alternates in a manner that includes comparative assessment of their respective goodness. Voluntary action and the exercise of free will are thus matters entirely within the defining individual notion of a substance, and have nothing to do with the fact that the existence of the substance depends upon the acts of God. It is in this sense that voluntary acts, albeit *determined,* are not *necessitated,* and that acts of will—like the events in the causal fabric of nature—have their sufficient reasons, which "incline without necessitating." Human freedom does not oppose predetermination or determination as such. The decision of the will is always a matter of preferential inclination: there can be no "freedom of indifference" of a will capable of resolving a choice between equally balanced and appealing alternatives. Yet our decision, though invariably *determined,* is exempt from constraint and from necessity,[30] for free action is a matter of the self-determining spontaneity of the spirits: the "inner necessity" of their *own* natures, resulting in acts that are their own, and in no way imposed or constrained. For Leibniz, human freedom is, as with Aristotle, the product of deliberation, judgment, and choice, whose authenticity is undisturbed by divine foreknowledge: if a future event is foreseen by the Creator, this does not mean that it will occur *because* it has been predicted by him. Nor is the fact that the complete individual notion or law of the individual series of a substance fixes all its properties and determines all events that will befall it constitute a block to its freedom, since this sort of determination is, according to Leibniz, to be viewed as a mode of self-determination, and thus exemplifies rather than impedes freedom.

---

[29] The causal overtones should be suppressed; we mean simply that it is the terminating member of a certain chain of events.

[30] "Freedom is as much exempt from *necessity* as from *constraint.* Neither the (determinate) futurity of truths, nor the foreknowledge and pre-ordination of God, nor the predisposition of things creates necessity" (*Causa Dei,* §102; *Phil.,* VI, p. 454).

Considering Leibniz' response to the first question, his way of dealing with the second becomes more apparent and plausible. The pivotal fact is that God does not make a substance what it is; indeed, *God is in no way responsible for what substances do*. When at first (so to speak) the substance subsists simply *sub ratione possibilitatis*, it is in God's mind simply as a conceptualized possibility over which He has no control; [31] He in no way determines the essence (nature) of an individual, although he invariably determines its existence. Even the best possible world will contain some imperfect substances—some grossly sinful men, for example. Their imperfection is embodied in their intrinsic nature (their complete individual notion), with which God has nothing to do. What He does have to do with—and this is the *only* aspect of the substance over which He exercises control—is the *existence* of the substance. He has to confront this choice on *systematic* grounds, between entire possible worlds, and not with respect to the merits or demerits of particular possible substances viewed in isolation.

Bertrand Russell has bitterly criticized Leibniz' ethical writings as being full of

> discreditable subterfuges to conceal the fact that *all* sin, for Leibniz, is original sin, the inherent finitude of any created monad. . . .[32]

The criticism is unjustified and unjust. Leibniz is, and there is no reason why Leibniz' readers should not be, perfectly aware of the fact at issue. What Leibniz wants to show, here as elsewhere, is that the technicalities of his system permit the standard distinctions to be drawn and the standard positions to be taken up. Just as reference to causal action and reaction can be accommodated in a world of windowless monads, the distinction between morality and immorality can be applied *within* the framework of agents totally pre-programmed by their defining individual notions. Leibniz is not attempting to conceal an alien ethic behind a surface of moral platitudes, but to show that an admittedly foreign and unaccustomed perspective can accommodate and make good sense of certain standard traditional views which he and his readers presumably agree in accepting.

---

31 The conceptual possibility simply "is what it is"—nothing (not even itself) "makes it be" that way. The various ethical considerations at issue here are canvassed carefully in the opuscule "Conversation sur la Liberté et sur le Destin" in G. Grua (ed.), *Textes inédits*, pp. 478-86.

32 Russell, *Critical Exposition*, p. 197.

twelve

THEODICY

The Nature and Existence of God

Leibniz repeatedly criticized Descartes and Spinoza for relying exclusively on one single argument for God's existence—the refurbished Ontological Argument of St. Anselm. He urged that other proofs, especially arguments that proceed from "the order of things," be used. Even if these wider-ranging reasonings should prove redundant from the exclusively rational point of view, they would prove of great use in helping to solidify the conviction of the ordinary man and "to silence the Atheist." Though perhaps not absolutely necessary, it is desirable to have a battery of diversified arguments for the existence of God. Leibniz himself gave special prominence to five different arguments: the Ontological Argument, the Cosmological Argument, the Argument from Eternal Truths, the Argument from Design, and the Modal Argument. We shall consider them in turn.[1]

---

[1] An interesting discussion of the historical development of Leibniz' views on proofs for the existence of God—essentially an evolution from early prime reliance upon the Ontological Argument to a late emphasis on what we have called the Modal Argument—can be found in Wolfgang Janke, "Das Ontologische Argument in der Frühzeit des Leibnizchen Denkins (1676–1678)," *Kantstudien,* vol. 54 (1963), pp. 259-87.

The Ontological Argument

The Ontological Argument reasons God's existence from His perfection. Starting with the definition of God as "the (all-)*perfect* being"—or alternatively as "the *most real* being"—it argues that *existence,* since it is a mode of perfection (or reality), must characterize this particular Being. Leibniz added one important qualification to this classical form of the argument. The line of reasoning involved attempts to elicit the necessity of its conclusion by inference from a premise which is, in effect, a definition. But, said Leibniz, a definition can be self-inconsistent, with the thing it purportedly defines actually impossible; "the fastest motion" and "the largest circle" were examples he gave. The Ontological Argument thus does no more than prove that, if God is possible, he exists. The question of possibility remains to be settled,[2] and another step is needed to render the argument cogent.

Leibniz employed several alternative reasonings to establish the possibility of a Being answering to the definition basic to the Ontological Argument. One takes the following form: the possibility of God follows *a posteriori* from the existence of contingent things. (This argument is developed at greater length below.) A second line of reasoning takes the more orthodox (i.e., traditional) form of maintaining that all modes of perfection are necessarily compatible with one another, so there could be no self-inconsistency in the idea of a Being which exhibits each of them in highest degree. The details of the reasoning are this. A *perfection* is, by definition, a quality that is 1) *simple* or absolute, and thus indefinable, and 2) positive and expresses its object without any restrictions or limitations. Two such qualities P and Q cannot possibly conflict when attributed to the same subject; incompatibility could arise only if they differ in direction (positivity or negativity), degree (i.e., extent), or resolutive constituents. But all of these possibilities are excluded by defining a quality as representing a perfection. Of course, if existence is included as a perfection in the sense of this definition, it will have to be classed as a quality, though of a very

---

[2] This objection had already been made to Descartes, and he replied to it in his answers to the second set of objectives to his *Meditations*. See V. Cousin, ed., *Oeuvres de Descartes,* Vol. I, pp. 407, 440 ff.

unusual nature. This is, as Kant was to remark, a major point of weakness in this argument.[3]

The Cosmological Argument (or the Argument from Sufficient Reason)

The starting point of the Cosmological Argument, as Leibniz states it, is not a definition or any sort of necessary premise, but a contingent fact: the existence of the world. Any particular happening in the world can always be explained in terms of its earlier states and the natural laws that govern its changes, but what of general questions regarding the nature of the world and its laws; why do things occur in the world as they do rather than otherwise? What is at issue is not the reason for any single member of the endless series of specific world states, but the reason for the whole series. Why are there any states at all? Why are they as they are rather than otherwise? Given the (logically necessary) Principle of Sufficient Reason, the whole series of world states must have a supermundane reason that lies outside itself. But the sufficient reason for the sphere of contingence must lie outside that sphere, in the sphere of the metaphysically necessary. Moreover, the reason for an existing thing must itself be an existing thing, thus the sufficient reason for the realm of contingence must be a metaphysically necessary existent—a Being whose essence involves existence—and this can only be God.[4]

Within its Leibnizian framework, the major limitations of this argument are twofold. First, it rests upon a purely factual premise—the existence of a range of contingents. This is a mild and venial failing, since the presupposition is not readily denied. The second, more serious, failing has to do with the *manner* in which the argument applies the Principle of Sufficient Reason: even if the applicability of the principle is conceded to Leibniz, his procedure

---

[3] It enmeshes the system of Leibniz in an apparent difficulty. The "logic of the system" is such that Leibniz is committed to exclude existence from the domain of qualities (properties) of things, it being crucially important to assure its nonoccurrence in the complete individual notions of things. Yet he seems to hold in one place that existence is a predicate (*Phil.*, V, pp. 339-40). However, this one solitary passage is not decisive. (Cf. footnote 16, p. 154.)

[4] *Phil.*, VII, p. 302.

in insisting upon locating the reason for the character of contingents in one unique existent external to the domain at issue still represents a questionable manner of application.

The Argument from Eternal Truths

This argument rests on the presupposition (it is no more than that, since Leibniz nowhere argues explicitly for its truth) that the eternal truths must have a locus of existence. The supposition seems to be that a truth cannot exist unthought, thus the existence of an eternal truth requires its location in the thought of an eternal thinker. Leibniz repeatedly describes God's understanding as the region of the eternal truths.[5] Man's recognition of certain truths as eternal is consequently deemed a sufficient basis for his inference to the existence of a Deity.

The Argument from Design

This is the ancient argument for the existence of God on the analogy with the human workman. As the plan and organization of the building attest to the arrangements of the master architect, so the great subtlety encountered in the works of nature attest the planning mind of the great Creator. The only characteristic touch Leibniz adds to the classic pattern of this reasoning has to do with the pre-established harmony. The endless coordination and mutual accommodation of existing substances cannot be accounted for except as the work of an all-knowing intellect. We can thus argue from the orderliness of the world,[6] and not simply from its existence, as with the Argument from Sufficient Reason, to the existence of a God in whom responsibility for this orderliness lies. The major weakness of the argument lies in its "exclusivity presupposition," to the effect that a certain feature of the universe (viz., its orderliness) is to be accounted for in only one conceivable way (viz., as the work of the Deity).

---

5 E.g., *Phil.*, VI, p. 115; VII, p. 311.
6 The argument thus also rests on a factual premise.

The Modal Argument

This characteristically Leibnizian proof of the existence of God is sometimes completely overlooked by commentators. It is, for example, quite put into the shade in Russell's emphasis, following that of Erdmann, upon the four aforementioned proofs offered by Leibniz.[7] The argument now at issue might well be termed the *Modal Argument,* for, like the Ontological Argument, it starts from a definition of God, but establishes His existence not by ordinary deduction but by *modal* reasoning.[8] We have already considered this argument in detail.[9]

God's Perfection and the Existence of Evil

Leibniz' Modal Argument for the existence of God leaves out entirely the issue of divine perfection, which has been considered in detail.[10]

God possesses the maximum amount of essence, and His acts (the sphere of His activity being the world) are the best possible. But while God's existence, and hence His metaphysical perfection is, as we have seen, necessary, His goodness as creator, i.e., His moral perfection, is contingent and the result of free choice.

We must now cope with the question of the relation between God's necessary metaphysical and His contingent moral perfection. In order to do this we must once more call to mind Leibniz' Prin-

---

[7] See pp. 172 ff. of Russell's *Critical Exposition,* and cf. J. E. Erdmann, *Geschichte der Philosophie,* Vol. II, pp. 168-69.

[8] That the argument we are about to consider was preferred by Leibniz over the others which he gave at times, and that it is this argument which he regarded as the most cogent was, to my knowledge, first pointed out by J. Iwanicki, *Leibniz et les démonstrations mathématiques de l'existence de Dieu* (Strasbourg: Librairie Universitaire d'Alsace, 1933), p. 207. Leibniz habitually supplemented his discussions of the Anselmio-Cartesian Ontological Argument by some such appendage as: "But even leaving out all mention of the divine perfection or grandeur, one can formulate the argument thus far in a more proper and rigorous fashion as follows . . ." (*Phil.,* IV, p. 359). What follows is the Modal Argument.

[9] See Chap. Five.

[10] See Chap. Five.

ciple of Sufficient Reason. As we have already seen, this asserts that every true proposition can be shown to be analytic by a (possibly infinite) process of "analysis" or "demonstration," i.e., a successive elimination of defined ideas by means of their definition. Using this principle, we can clarify the logical relation between the two types of divine perfection. God's moral perfection (goodness) has a sufficient reason, and this in turn another, *et cetera ad infinitum;* but this sequence of sufficient reasons converges on God's metaphysical perfection.[11] Or, putting this another way, we can say that God's moral perfection is indeed a logical consequence of His metaphysical perfection, but a consequence which no finite deduction suffices to elicit. In this way, as Leibniz insists, the proposition asserting God's moral perfection is contingent; God is good by free choice, not necessitation.

It is precisely the infinite regress which Russell invokes in his *reductio ad absurdum* of Leibniz' contention that God's goodness is contingent which establishes this contingence.

Leibniz distinguishes [12] three modes of evil: *physical* evil, which consists of suffering, *moral* evil, sin, and *metaphysical* evil, the imperfection of creatures. The first two reduce to the third, for if God admits evil into creation, to create it as such would contravene God's own perfection. Evil of any sort cannot properly be said to be *created* by God; [13] rather it is *admitted into existence* by him as an unavoidable concomitant of the perfections he seeks to realize in creation.

In his doctrine of contingence, perhaps more heavily than in any other part of his philosophy, Leibniz the philosopher is indebted to Leibniz the mathematician. The logic underlying this doctrine stems entirely and directly from Leibniz' mathematical investigations:

> There is something which had me perplexed for a long time—how it is possible for the predicate of a proposition to be contained in (*inesse*) the subject without making the proposition necessary. But

---

[11] This is so since the (infinite) analysis of the contingent *must* ultimately lead to the necessary, i.e., to God *qua* metaphysically perfect (*Phil.,* VII, p. 200). It it because he holds this that Leibniz, speaking now in the language not of truths but of things, maintains, "If there were no necessary being, there would be no contingent being" (*Phil.,* VII, p. 310).

[12] *Phil.,* VI, p. 115; *Théodicée,* §21.

[13] See *Causa Dei,* §§68-71; *Phil.,* VI, pp. 449-50.

the knowledge of Geometrical matters, and especially of infinitesimal analysis, lit the lamp for me, so that I came to see that notions too can be resolvable *in infinitum*.[14]

At length some new and unexpected light appeared from a direction in which my hopes were smallest—from *mathematical* considerations regarding the nature of the infinite. In truth there are two labyrinths in the human mind, one concerning the composition of the continuum, the other concerning the nature of freedom. And both of these spring from exactly the same source—the infinite.[15]

Against this background it becomes possible to appreciate Leibniz' exculpation of God from blame for evil and imperfection as they seem to exist in the world. Each substance has always subsisted (or, strictly speaking, has had being outside of time altogether) *sub ratione possibilitatis* in the mind of God. Its total nature was determined, for its adequate and complete notion (i.e., all of its predicates save existence) was fixed.[16] For this nature God is in no way responsible; it is an object of his understanding, and no creature of his will. God chose for actualization the best, i.e., most perfect, system of compossible substances; He is the reason for all existence, hence for all existent perfection and imperfection. Imperfection is not avoidable since, by the identity of indiscernibles, no substance different from God can be wholly perfect. God, however, chose to minimize imperfection (or, positively, to maximize perfection), thus He is positively the cause of existent perfection, but only negatively of imperfection, since He retained only what could not but remain.

---

14 Couturat, *Opuscules,* p. 18.

15 Couturat, *Logique,* p. 210, notes.

16 "The complete or perfect notion of a singular substance involves all its predicates, past, present, and future" (Couturat, *Opuscules,* p. 520; cf. *ibid.,* p. 403). That existence is not among these predicates follows from the fact that the complete notion of the possible substances was completely determined and accessible to the mind of God anterior to any decisions of creation (cf. *Phil.,* II, p. 50). It is therefore clear that existence, if a predicate at all for Leibniz, is a very exceptional one. Thus Leibniz remarks on the margin of a manuscript which cannot possibly antedate 1686: "If existence were anything other than what essence demands, then it would follow that it has an essence of some sort, and would add something new to things, of which one might in turn ask whether this essence exists, and why this [exists] rather than something else" (*Phil.,* VII, p. 195, n.b.). And I by no means agree with Russell, who regards *Phil.,* V, p. 339, as establishing conclusively that Leibniz held existence to be a predicate (Russell, *Critical Exposition,* pp. 27, 174, 185). Indeed, in this passage Leibniz seems to be concerned to reduce existence from the status of a real characteristic to that of an *ens rationis,* like relations. (Cf. footnote 3, p. 150.)

God has no choice but to tolerate the evils that are an inevitable consequence of the good that is the primary object of his will; He

> . . . is willing to permit them [unavoidable evils] for a greater good. . . . This is a *consequent* will, resulting from acts of *antecedent* will, in which one wills the good.[17]

Leibniz is not in a position to translate the lack of *necessity* in what happens in the world into a lack of *inevitability*. In a larger sense, embracing moral as well as metaphysical considerations, he must admit that things in the actual world "could not have been otherwise" than in fact they are. However, this inevitably is not of a logico-metaphysical but of a *moral* character, and replaces fatalistic determinism by a moralistic finalism turning on the perfection of the things that exist in this world, rather than upon the inherent necessity of its laws. This is how Leibniz accounts for imperfection in the best of all possible worlds.

Leibniz envisages that an objection can be made to the idea of a "best possible universe" on grounds that it is impossible to conceive of a *best* creature of any kind; it will always be possible to imagine a more perfect one, and so on *ad indefinitum*.[18] This objection, he maintains, is not correct, since it does not apply to the type of "creature" that is an entire universe, and what may hold for an individual substance will not hold for a universe:

> Someone will say that it is impossible to produce the best [possible world] because there is no perfect creature, and that it is always possible to produce one still more perfect. I reply that what can be said of a creature or of a particular substance, which can be surpassed always by another, is not to be applied to the universe, which, since it must extend through all future eternity, is an infinity.[19]

The City of God

The monads of the highest grade, the spirits, alone share with God in both the intellectual capacity for self-consciousness and the

---

17 *Phil.*, VI, p. 382. *Summary of the Controversy of the "Théodicée" Reduced to Formal Arguments*, Reply to Objection IV.
18 This anticipates a line of argument later espoused by Kant in his *Versuch einiger Betrachtungen über den Optimismus* (1759).
19 *Phil.*, VI, p. 232; *Théodicée*, §195.

moral capacity for reasoned choice based on a vision of the good. Whereas all monads mirror the created world of other monads, the spirits are a reflection, albeit a pale one, of God as well. The spirits comprise the City of God:

> . . . this truly universal monarchy, [which] is a moral world within the natural world, and [is] the highest and most divine of the works of God. It is in this [sphere] that the glory of God truly consists, for He would have none of His greatness and goodness, were they not admired by spirits. It is, too, in relation to this divine city that He properly has goodness: whereas His wisdom and power are manifest everywhere.[20]

The welfare of the spirits is, as discussed already, a prime consideration with God: "There is no room for doubt that the felicity of the spirits is the principal aim of God and that He puts this purpose into execution as far as the general harmony will permit." [21] But even God cannot exclude the moral evil of spirits from the best possible world (this is the root of original sin for Leibniz), for God has no control over an evil that inheres in the definitive nature of a spirit. Hence:

> The grace of God, whether ordinary or extraordinary, has its degrees and its measures. It is always of itself . . . sufficient not only to keep one from sin but even to effect his salvation, provided that a man does his part in cooperating with it. It [i.e., God's grace] has not always, however, sufficient power to overcome a man's inclination, for if it did it would no longer be limited in any way. . . .[22]

His eagerness to assign a special status to spirits within the realm of monads leads Leibniz into some of the more remote reaches of his system. Every monad has its continuing historical self-identity, as codified in its complete individual notion and concretized in its present reflection of its past states. But spirits exhibit not only the continuing metaphysical self-identity of all created substances but also a moral self-identity. Cosmic history is so arranged that a spirit never descends to the level of a bare monad; it always has a body, i.e., is the dominant monad of an organically structured aggregate. No matter how low this may descend on the organic scale, a spirit always, throughout its whole history, qualifies for membership in the community of morally qualified individuals.

---

20 *Monadology*, §86. Cf. PNG, §§14-15.
21 *Phil.*, IV, p. 430; *Discourse on Metaphysics*, §5.
22 *Phil.*, IV, pp. 455-56; *Discourse on Metaphysics*, §30.

God performs miracles especially for the sake of the spirits over whom he presides as monarch. Leibniz explains in his correspondence with Clarke that a "miracle" is any art which, like the creation itself, "surpasses the powers of creatures." [23] The acts of divine choice aimed to assure the benefit of the spirits are miraculous, but that does not make them arbitrary or inexplicable:

> As God can do nothing without reasons, even when He acts miraculously, it follows that He has no will about individual events but what results from some general truth or will. Thus I would say that God never has a *particular will* . . . i.e., a *particular primitive will.* I think even that miracles have nothing to distinguish them from other events in this regard: for reasons of an order superior to that of Nature [i.e., the "common course of nature"] prompt God to perform them.[24]

Cosmic Evolution and Melioration

Leibniz discusses, without committing himself, the possibility of a first instant, prior to all others both in time and in nature. By his own statement this question of a first instant is closely allied with the changes of the state of perfection of the universe:

> One may form two hypotheses, the one that nature is always equally perfect, the other that it always grows in perfection. If it [nature] is always equally perfect [as a whole], but variable [in the parts], it is more probable that there was no beginning [of the universe]. But if it always grows in perfection (assuming that it is not possible to give it all its perfection at once) the question may again be explicated in two ways. . . .[25]

These two ways are 1) a growth of perfection from all eternity which, since it has not come to an end, must be asymptotic; and 2) an increase of perfection starting from a fixed instant of creation. Leibniz arrives at no final conclusion, and concludes his discussion saying: "I do not yet see a way to show demonstratively which [solution] one ought to choose according to pure reason." [26] In his fifth letter to Clarke, Leibniz writes:

---

23 *Phil.*, VII, p. 416 (5th letter to Clarke, §107).
24 *Phil.*, VI, pp. 240-41; *Théodicée*, §§206-7.
25 *Phil.*, III, p. 582.
26 *Loc. cit.*

If the nature of things as a whole is to grow uniformly in perfection, the universe of creatures must have had a beginning.[27] Thus it is more reasonable to postulate a beginning for it than to admit limits for it, in order to secure . . . the character of an infinite Author.[28]

But here too Leibniz does not commit himself.[29]

Although Leibniz hesitates, for lack of final proof, to be dogmatic in regard to the quantity of past time or change in the relative perfection of the universe, he personally inclines, with respect to the latter question, toward an increase. Here, as elsewhere, we find a dynamic tendency in Leibniz' thought; he clearly prefers the idea of a developing plan of campaign, a continuing project, to that of an architect's plan, a static picture. His grounds for inclination toward a growth in perfection are in the psychological observation that human happiness lies in the anticipation of greater future goods.[30] It is because in its changes a monad approaches asymptotically a final high point of perfection that the analogy between Leibniz' *appetition* and Spinoza's *conatus* cannot be pressed, as some interpreters have inclined to do. We see here, once again, Leibniz' tendency to insist on metaphysical counterparts to an ethical theme:

> As for the afflictions, especially of good men, however, we must take it as assured that these lead to their greater good and that this is true not only theologically but also naturally. . . . In general, one may say that, though afflictions are temporary evils, they are good in effect, for they are shortcuts to greater perfection. . . . We may call this backing up the better to spring forward ("qu'on recule pour mieux sauter").[31]

This inclination toward a theory of cosmic melioration is one of the striking characteristics of Leibniz' optimism. It is distinctly a decorative feature added to the basic structure of his philosophy, not an inexorable consequence of the fundamental position of his

---

27 Here the use of "uniformement" rules out the asymptotic possibility.
28 *Phil.*, VII, p. 408 (5th letter to Clarke, §74).
29 The themes treated in this section are developed extensively in two brief memoranda: *De progressu in infinitum* (1694/1696?) in Grua (ed.), *Textes inédits*, pp. 94-95; and *An mundus perfectione crescat*, found in *ibid.*, p. 95.
30 ". . . our happiness will never consist, and ought not to consist, in a full enjoyment, in which there would be nothing further to desire, and which would render our spirit stupid, but rather in a perpetual advance (progrès) to new pleasures and new perfections" (*Phil.*, VI, p. 606).
31 *Phil.*, VII, pp. 307-8.

system. Leibniz' exposition of the nature of the spirits, their place in the metaphysical order, and their destiny in cosmic history is one of the few, and interestingly revealing, loose points of his otherwise tightly structured system. It is a forced move, rather than one of intrinsic necessity, to pivot Leibniz' metaphysic about a conception of a final cause of the universe in terms of a progress toward perfection in the community of spirits.

Excursus

Modern commentators tend to remark disparagingly upon the striking contrast of Leibniz' system between its daringly innovative logic, epistemology, and metaphysics and its extremely conservative ethics and theology. (Similar complaints are sometimes lodged against Descartes.) Bertrand Russell has even suggested that Leibniz had two systems: "the good philosophy which he had kept to himself, and . . . the vulgarized version by which he won the admiration of Princes and (even more) of Princesses." [32] This view of the matter seems to me wholly unjustified. Quite the reverse seems true: the guiding aim and aspiration of Leibniz' philosophy is to establish a rigorous rational foundation for what he accepted as the fundamental teachings of ethics and theology. To do this in detail and provide the means for a solid demonstration of "the conformity of faith with reason" took Leibniz into the construction of a highly novel philosophy. But its novelties were not introduced for their own sake—his is the case of a man who feels himself constrained to use uncommon means to achieve a familiar, commonplace destination. His immensely penetrative intelligence led Leibniz to the construction of a highly unorthodox theory, but he never concealed from himself the fact (which we too must realize) that the purpose of this theory was to provide a conceptually solid underpinning for certain essentially orthodox views in ethics and theology.

It is surprising to what extent Leibniz brought himself to a belief that the orthodox character of his ends could get his readers to accept the unusual route by which he reached them. The correspondence with Arnauld on the nature of substance and that with Des

---

32 Russell, *Critical Exposition*, p. vi.

Bosses on transubstantiation bear remarkable evidence of this. Leibniz genuinely believed that if an intellectually secure foundation for ethics and theology were provided, men would be brought together. This optimistic goal was one he never gave up, even in the face of endless discouragements.

Leibniz eagerly wanted to persuade his readers (usually his correspondents), not in order to win personal disciples in high places, but to secure effective adherents to implement a vision of truths which he felt capable of healing the theological strifes and political discords in Europe of his day. Had fame been his prime goal he would have written more books and fewer letters. What Leibniz wanted was not public acclaim, but influential converts who could implement in the sphere of action his reconciling insights in the sphere of thought. It is always risky to speculate on motives, but in my own mind there is no doubt that the aspirations which actuated him were, in the main, not those of selfishness but of public spirit.

INDEX OF NAMES

SUBJECT INDEX

A

Action, 83-84, 145-47
Actual Infinite, 107, 112
Aggregation, 82, 114, 123
Akademie der Wissenschaften (Berlin), 4
Altdorf, University of, 2
Analysis, 23-29, 40-43
Analysis situs, 100-101
Analytic propositions, 25-26, 31-33
Anselm, ontological argument of, 11, 66-67, 148, 149-50
Apperception, 125-26, 130, 134-35
Appetition, 59-63, 119, 158
Argument from design, 151
Argument from eternal truths, 66, 151
Argument from the pre-established harmony, 66-67

B

Bare monads, 118-19
Best possible world, 19, 140-41, 155
Brachistochrone problem, 41-43

C

Calculating machines, 3
Calculus, 3, 4, 31, 38, 40, 42, 43, 45, 112, 131
Calculus ratiocinator, 131-32
Calculus of variations, 31
Causality, 61-63, 83-84, 104
City of God, 119, 139-41, 155-57
Clearness of perception, 63
Coexistence, 92
Common sensibles, 130

164

71
12

74
75
76
79

83
86
88